Here's what others are saying about Face to Face

"At the end of the day (make that the end of your life!) your personal relationship with God is just that. Personal. And relational. It's about you and God. No one or no thing else. Not you and your job. Not you and your family. Not even you and your marriage. Only you and Him. Alone together. It stands to reason you need some quality time Face to Face."

—Stu Weber, Author of *Tender Warrior*

"Like a great coach who can take you farther than you can take yourself, Monte Kline's *Face to Face* lays out a game plan for a deeper and more meaningful relationship with Christ – one that focuses the mind and centers the heart on Jesus."

—Tom Flick, Motivational Speaker and
Former NFL Quarterback

Our ministry is getting people to "come apart" in groups, but the real work is accomplished one by one. Monte Kline's book is a rich treasure house of guidance for individually facing God through retreat.

—David R. Talbott, Associate Director of Advancement
Mount Hermon Christian Camps & Conference
Center, Mount Hermon, California

Face to Face

MEETING GOD IN THE QUIET PLACES

You should be longing to climb the hill of the Lord,
desiring to see Him face to face.

– Charles Spurgeon

by

Monte Kline

Intermedia Publishing Group

Face to Face
MEETING GOD IN THE QUIET PLACES

Published by:
Intermedia Publishing Group, Inc.
P.O. Box 2825
Peoria, Arizona 85380
www.intermediapub.com

ISBN 978-1-935529-62-0

Unless otherwise noted, scripture references are taken from the English Standard Version of The Holy Bible published by Crossway Bibles, a division of Good News Publishers, Wheaton, Illinois.

Table of Contents

Introduction

There are times when solitude is better than company and silence is wiser than speech.

— Charles Spurgeon

I don't remember for sure when my first "face to face" meeting with God took place. But one day I decided it would be a good idea to get in the car and take off for a day, or two or four to some isolated spot and just have what I call a "Personal Retreat" with him. What happened changed my life then and continues to change my life now. I entered a whole new realm of Christian experience. This book reflects what God taught me in many Personal Retreat encounters.

So what is a Personal Retreat?

A Personal Retreat is a special time away to meet with God for the purpose of deepening your relationship with him as you seek his illumination and direction for your life.

A Personal Retreat combines spiritual disciplines of solitude, simplicity, prayer, meditation, confession and worship. Though not by that name, we find this concept throughout the Bible.

Encounters with God through Personal Retreats have carried me through the most excruciatingly difficult times in my life. The pain of life forced me to seek God in a deeper way than just a morning quiet time, an uplifting worship service, a Bible study or a powerful sermon. I knew a lot of things *about* God before I did Personal Retreats, but through those many "face to face" encounters, I am beginning to actually *know* God.

So do you *know* God, or do you really *know* God? Paul came to know Christ at his conversion on the Damascus Road, at least to know him in the sense of eternal salvation. Yet 25 years later, near the end of his life, writing from a Roman prison cell he pleads:

> . . . *that I may know him and the power of his resurrection, and may share his sufferings, becoming like him in his death . . . (Phil. 3:10)*

As Christians we know him, but we can know him more and more in an ever-growing intimate relationship. Personal Retreats provide one way of developing that intimacy.

The goal of this book is simple: to lead you into a life of "face to face" meetings with God – encounters after which you will never be the same.

Chapter One

Missing Thirst

I help people become thirsty. In 25 years as a health practitioner, I've counseled thousands of people to drink pure water and to drink more of it – people like Sandy. Complaining of fatigue, depression and skin problems, Sandy sought a more natural way to solve her health problems than just popping more prescription drugs. Where I asked on our information form, "How much water do you drink daily," she checked 0 – 16 oz., at best one-fourth her needed intake. Like a lot of people, Sandy was drinking hardly any water at all, much to the demise of her health. But why? When I asked why she drank so little water, she gave the usual reply, "I'm just not thirsty." Why are some people thirsty, while most are falsely satiated?

More importantly, why are some Christians *spiritually* thirsty and others not? Why do some attend a Sunday morning service receiving a spoonful of inspirational water, yet be indifferent toward a Bible study, a home fellowship, a seminar or a time of prayer and fasting? Why are some Christians seemingly thirsty for so little of Jesus Christ, while others cry from the depths of their heart with the Psalmist:

As the deer pants for the flowing streams, so pants my soul for you, O God. My soul thirsts for God, for the living God. (Ps. 42:1-2a)

O God, you are my God; earnestly I seek you; my soul thirsts for you; my flesh faints for you, as in a dry and weary land where there is no water. (Ps. 63:1)

Personal Retreats are only for the thirsty. For anyone else, they're a waste of time. There's nothing magical or mechanical about these special times alone with God. It's not a gimmick to gain insight or power. The right heart attitude produces success in the endeavor. Therefore we must begin with the question of thirst. Do you have it? And, if you don't, how do you get it?

INVITATION TO THE THIRSTY

God invites the thirsty to an intimate relationship with himself:

Come, everyone who thirsts, come to the waters. (Isa. 55:1a)

If you knew the gift of God, and who it is that is saying to you, "Give me a drink," you would have asked him, and he would have given you living water . . . Everyone who drinks of this water will be thirsty again, but whoever drinks of the water that I will give him will never be thirsty forever. The water that I will give him will become in him a spring of water welling up to eternal life. (John 4:10, 13-14)

If anyone thirsts, let him come to me and drink. Whoever believes in me, as the Scripture has said, "Out of his heart will flow rivers of living water." (John 7:37b-38)

And he said to me, "It is done! I am the Alpha and the Omega, the beginning and the end. To the thirsty I will give from the spring of the water of life without payment." (Rev. 21:6)

The Spirit and the Bride say, "Come." And let the one who hears say, "Come." And let the one who is thirsty come; let the one who desires take the water of life without price. (Rev. 22:17)

What generous invitations to drink, yet most of us only take a sip. Where is the thirst that would "drive us to drink?"

A DRINKING PROBLEM?

In the spoof movie, *Airplane*, actor Robert Hays repeatedly pours water all over himself when he brings a glass to his mouth explaining, "I have a drinking problem." The humor makes a serious point: drinking is a developed skill. Christians have this "drinking" problem – we must **learn** to drink. But **drinking also assumes thirst.** If you're not thirsty, why bother to drink? As the old adage says, "You can lead a horse to water, but you can't make him drink." However, you can feed him salt . . . later we'll look at how God does just that with us.

CHRISTIANS LACKING THIRST

So why do so many Christians lack spiritual thirst? The Prophet Jeremiah identified perhaps the primary cause:

Be appalled, O heavens, at this; be shocked, be utterly desolate, declares the Lord, for my people have committed two evils: they have forsaken me, the fountain of living waters, and hewed out cisterns for themselves, broken cisterns that can hold no water. (Jer. 2:12-13)

God stands utterly amazed in this passage calling on the heavens to be shocked and desolate! When God is incredulous, we should take note. How could his children *refuse* his provision, his fountain, his "living water" to instead provide for themselves from much inferior cisterns? And what did they choose instead of the refreshment of an intimate relationship with God? They chose their own fulfillment apart from God. What delusion!

To say that choosing a cistern for your water supply over a fountain is dumb is to put it mildly. Cisterns haven't really changed much over the centuries. I remember one my grandfather had when I was little kid. You have to understand Ira Kline, born in 1880, never quite embraced the twentieth century. He wouldn't change his clocks to Daylight Savings Time as he laughed saying, "You can't change the sun!" His house had a coal stove for heat in the middle of the linoleum-floored dining room, an outhouse I once got locked into (haven't been really keen on outhouses since), plastic covering over the windows for the Midwest winter (didn't bother to remove in summer) and running water – *if you pumped hard enough!* That hand pump next to the kitchen sink was connected to a cistern, which got its water from the rain gutters draining into it.

Do you get excited about drinking water out of an old, moldy brick or concrete tank full of water that ran off the roof and through your gutters? Cistern water probably would not be your first choice. But a broken cistern? Now that's really crazy! Yet, metaphorically speaking, that's what the Israelites chose over God's fountain of living water. But have we learned the lesson today? Probably not. We continue to choose the broken cistern over the fountain.

OUR BROKEN CISTERNS

Thirst is real – you have to do something about it, but will you chose a broken cistern or God's fountain? Emptiness in our lives is real; you have to do something about it, whether a man-provided remedy or a God-provided one. Philosopher Blaise Pascal said:

> *What is it, then, that this desire and this inability proclaim to us, but that there was once in man a true happiness of which there now remain to him only the mark and empty trace, which he in vain tries to fill from all his surroundings, seeking from things absent the help he does not obtain in things present? But these are all inadequate, because the infinite abyss can only be filled by an infinite and immutable object, that is to say, only by God himself.[1]*

So what do we fill our broken spiritual cisterns with? Certainly not *spiritual* remedies. Rather, we attempt

5

to fill Pascal's God-shaped vacuum with *physical* and *mental* remedies:

1. Materialism – The pursuit of "stuff" – bigger and newer houses, cars, boats, planes, clothes; things Jesus warned, "moth and rust destroys" and "thieves break in and steal" (Matt. 6:19). We start out owning our toys, but in the end they own us. The fact that these *may* represent legitimate needs misses the point – they can never fill the spiritual void left by lack of intimacy with God. Solomon nailed our problem in these words:

> *When goods increase, they increase who eat them, and what advantage has their owner but to see them with his eyes?* (Eccles. 5:11)

2. Money & Success – Are there Christians who thirst for money and success as they should only thirst for Christ's living water? Of course. Climbing the ladder, building the career, more and more, better and better, they ceaselessly strive. Yet how fleeting is that success. But are we then supposed to be failures? Hardly. Money and success are legitimate in their proper place, but they too are transitory and empty of spiritual value. Again we read in Ecclesiates:

> *He who loves money will not be satisfied with money, nor he who loves wealth with his income; this also is vanity.* (Eccles. 5:10)

3. Food – Do you "live to eat" or "eat to live?" As a practicing nutritionist, I tend to notice what people look like as they walk by on the street. It's not a pretty picture! Probably half or more of the population suffers from weight problems. This cannot be exclusively blamed on our gluttonous culture, but it is partly the result of it. Ever watched people chow down in buffet restaurants where you'll see the most grossly obese people pile food on their plate (after plate) like there's no tomorrow? They're not eating because of true physical hunger. More often, gluttony is simply a vain attempt to feel good emotionally and spiritually. We need to eat, but filling a spiritual vacuum with food is futile.

4. Sex – We had to get to sex eventually, right? Sex within God's designed boundaries is not only wonderful, but also necessary to survival. But no matter how pleasurable for the moment, it cannot make a spiritually empty person full, even when within God's design of marriage. Physical, emotional and spiritual damage typically result when sex is used outside of his design.

None of these examples is evil in itself when used as God intended. But to center one's life on these "broken cisterns" and to think they will produce a deep and lasting satisfaction, a peace and a spiritual fulfillment is ridiculous. God offers a fountain of living water for our spiritual thirst, but will we receive it?

CHEAP GRACE

Christians lack thirst due to what German pastor and World War II martyr, Dietrich Bonhoeffer, called "cheap grace." It's not a new problem. Paul addressed it in Romans:

> *What shall we say then? Are we to continue in sin that grace may abound? By no means! How can we who died to sin still live in it?* (Rom. 6:1-2)

New Testament references to "cheap grace" highlight the idea of viewing grace as a license to sin. Yet today's "cheap grace" manifests more as a license to complacency, to laziness, to an "all's well in Zion" attitude among Christians who are comfortable.

"Comfortable" is not part of the Christian lexicon. If we're here to be "comfortable," what's the point of our earthly existence? Why didn't God just put us in Heaven in the first place? Because that would not fulfill his purpose of conforming us to the image of Christ through the battle he has placed us in on this planet. God didn't drop us into a comfortable picnic but into a war, for "the Lord is a Warrior" (Exod. 15:3). Look at the Scripture:

For you, O God, have tested us; you have tried us as silver is tried. You brought us into the net; you laid a crushing burden on our backs; you let men ride over our heads; we went through fire and through water; yet you have brought us out to a place of abundance. (Ps. 66:10-12)

Give ear to my prayer, O God, and hide not yourself from my plea for mercy! Attend to me, and answer me; I am restless in my complaint and I moan, because of the noise of the enemy, because of the oppression of the wicked. For they drop trouble upon me, and in anger they bear a grudge against me. (Ps. 55:1-3)

He redeems my soul in safety from the battle that I wage, for many are arrayed against me. God will give ear and humble them, he who is enthroned from of old, because they do not change and do not fear God. (Ps. 55:18-19)

Deliver me from sinking in the mire; let me be delivered from my enemies and from the deep waters. (Ps. 69:14)

A book could be filled with references to the enemies and battles we fight. I have been surrounded by enemies from the beginning of my Christian life forty years ago. Yet the number of Christians that have known no such war stuns me. Their health is good, their income secure, kids are doing fine, they don't have an enemy in the world. . . and they lack the desperate thirst required for a Personal Retreat. To which I'm tempted to scream, "What's wrong with you!" If the kingdom of darkness finds nothing worthy of attacking you for, perhaps it's time to reconsider exactly what kind of Christianity you are practicing.

Christian psychologist, Larry Crabb, says that cheap grace:

> . . . *develops when we talk about grace before we tremble at God's holiness.*[2]

You see, contemporary Christians aren't just comfortable with life; they're also comfortable with God. There's a fine line to walk here. We have been brought close to God through the blood of Christ. Jesus is our friend (John 15:15) and brother. We can boldly come to the throne of grace (Heb. 4:16). But that grace, says Crabb, will become cheap if we do not *first* "tremble at his holiness."

As the Elect of God we were chosen in him before the foundation of the world (Eph. 1:4). By grace we were saved, through faith, not as a result of works (Eph. 2:8-9), for no work we could do could merit God's righteousness. But after we're spiritually regenerated, we are called to sanctification – to working out what God has worked in, as the Apostle Paul exhorts the Philippians:

> *Therefore, my beloved, as you have always obeyed, so now, not only as in my presence but much more in my absence, work out your own salvation with*

fear and trembling, for it is God who works in you, both to will and to work for his good pleasure. (Phil. 2:12-13)

No cheap grace here, for the holiness of God is being contemplated.

WORSHIPPING AN UNKNOWN GOD

Not truly *knowing* God is yet another reason for our lack of spiritual thirst. Sadly few Christians seriously study the Person of God to really know who he is, to know what he is like. Rather than worship the real thing, they are stuck with a caricature of God composed of:

(1) Some Old Testament "shadow" (Heb. 10:1; Col. 2:17)
(2) Some New Testament "substance" (Col. 2:17)
(3) Lots of the "traditions of men" (Mark 7:8)

We say we "know God" relative to having received Christ for salvation, but do we really *know* him? Do we know who he is and what he is like? Do we know him as we know a friend we have known for years? The Lord said through Jeremiah:

Let not the wise man boast in his wisdom, let not the mighty man boast in his might, let not the rich man boast in his riches, but let him who boasts boast in this, that he understands and knows me, that I am the Lord who practices steadfast love, justice, and righteousness in the earth. For in these things I delight, declares the Lord. (Jer. 9:23-24)

Recently at my church, I taught an Adult Sunday School class on "The Attributes of God" spending thirteen weeks studying God's self-existence, eternity, transcendence, immanence, immutability, omniscience, omnipotence, wisdom, goodness, severity, justice, grace, mercy, love, holiness and sovereignty. Just preparing for the classes was one of the most deepening experiences of my Christian life. But the amazing thing was how many in the class left with a very different concept of God than they came in with. It can be quite a shock to find out, after years of being a Christian, that you really don't know God! In our day we just don't study the Person of God the way the Puritans did, for example. Our lack of depth and devotion compared to theirs testifies of our failure.

SPIRITUAL APATHY

Why do so many Christians lack spiritual thirst? Could it also be plain apathy? Too many believers just don't care. In some cases they just haven't fully surrendered their lives to Christ; in other cases they may not even be truly converted. Whatever the reason, spiritual apathy blocks spiritual progress and therefore, spiritual depth. To not care is to not be thirsty. To not be thirsty is to never come into an intimate relationship with God.

So (1) How do we get thirsty and (2) How do we learn to drink?

THE CREATION OF THIRST

God not only invites the thirsty to drink, but **he makes them thirsty!** In fact, life might be seen as a giant divine conspiracy designed to make us thirsty. God's plan is to conform us to the image of Christ (Rom. 8:29). Because he is sovereign and wise, everything fulfills his plans, even life in a fallen world where things never go totally the way we think they should. We live in a world of bad weather and weeds and toil and things that break and people that betray us. No matter how hard we try to make our life "perfect," the fly always appears in the ointment. Solomon lamented:

> *Vanity of vanities, says the Preacher, vanity of vanities! All is vanity. What does man gain by all the toil at which he toils under the sun . . . Consider the work of God: who can make straight what he has made crooked?* (Eccles. 1:2-3;7:13)

We are sovereignly afflicted.

BROCCOLI OR ICE CREAM?

How many kids, given the choice of eating broccoli or ice cream, would choose the broccoli? Not many, maybe not any. But because of people called parents, who know what is required for healthy growth, kids are often forced to eat broccoli and only later get the ice cream. Good parents don't allow their kids to pick their own diet, as much as their kids wish they would.

Comedian Bill Cosby tells a hilarious story in one of his routines about being asked by his wife to fix breakfast for their youngest daughter. She notices a chocolate cake on the counter and proceeds to beg Dad to give her chocolate cake for breakfast. Cosby begins a perverse reasoning about the ingredients of the chocolate cake: This contains milk, wheat, eggs – sounds just like breakfast! Low and behold, his daughter gets chocolate cake for breakfast . . . and then Mom comes in and raises the roof!

It may be hard to imagine a parent being conned into giving their child chocolate cake for breakfast, but it's not hard to imagine Christians asking their Father for spiritual chocolate cake. Give me that prosperity, that worldly success, those material goods, disease-free health and the like! Unlike Bill Cosby, though, God is not conned by our immature petitions for that which does not nourish us. He gives us a life of spiritual bran to cleanse us and spiritual proteins to sustain us. Plus he keeps life just fouled up enough to keep us coming back to him – to keep us thirsty. In his great compassion and love to bring us to spiritual adulthood, he orders our path:

> *The steps of a man are established by the Lord, when he delights in his way; though he fall, he shall not be cast headlong, for the Lord upholds his hand.* (Ps. 37:23-34)

BENEFITS OF AFFLICTION

Tell me how thirsty you are for God, and I'll tell you how much affliction you've experienced. Thirst and affliction are inseparable. Affliction is the norm for Christians:

> *Many are the afflictions of the righteous, but the Lord delivers him out of them all.* (Ps. 34:19)

> *How long, O Lord? Will you forget me forever? How long will you hide your face from me? How long must I take counsel in my soul and have sorrow in my heart all the day? How long shall my enemy be exalted over me?* (Ps. 13:1-2)

Before I was afflicted I went astray, but now I keep your word. (Ps. 119:67)

It is good for me that I was afflicted, that I might learn your statutes. (Ps. 119:71)

I know, O Lord, that your rules are righteous, and that in faithfulness you have afflicted me. (Ps. 119:75)

In this you rejoice, though now for a little while, if necessary, you have been grieved by various trials, so that the tested genuineness of your faith—more precious than gold that perishes though it is tested by fire—may be found to result in praise and glory and honor at the revelation of Jesus Christ. (1 Pet. 1:6-7)

Beloved, do not be surprised at the fiery trial when it comes upon you to test you, as though something strange were happening to you. But rejoice insofar as you share Christ's sufferings, that you may also rejoice and be glad when his glory is revealed. (1 Pet. 4:12-13)

And after you have suffered a little while, the God of all grace, who has called you to his eternal glory in Christ will himself restore, confirm, strengthen, and establish you. To him, be the dominion forever and ever. Amen. (1 Pet. 5:10)

So what is God really doing in our lives through affliction, through all the suffering? There's the rub. We fallaciously assume God wants to **do** something through us, when really all God wants is to **do** something **in** us. Pastor Rick Warren in *The Purpose Driven Life* says:

> *God is far more interested in what you are than in what you do. We are human **beings**, not human **doings**.*[3]

God has only one business – making man in his image. He started doing that with the first Adam; he continues by remaking us into his image through the second Adam, Jesus Christ. Everything God does in our lives simply serves to conform us to the image of Christ. Because God is infinitely wise we can know that nothing but affliction will accomplish this goal. If there was another way, he would have used it. Affliction ideally destroys all the false "thirst quenchers" of life, replacing them with a true thirst for God alone.

RECIPE FOR THIRST

If you're already thirsty, you don't need this recipe. But if you're like most of us, you know you don't have the spiritual thirst you should have. So how do we get thirsty? Here are some steps:

1. Stop making "broken cisterns." Embrace your emptiness and let it drive you to the Lord. Cease trying to fill your "God-shaped vacuum" with the stuff of this world, as you realize you were created for another world. Stop dodging the suffering. Stop trying to be your own savior making your life "suffer-proof." I love the J. B. Phillips paraphrase of James 1:2-4:

When all kinds of trials and temptations crowd into your lives, my brothers, don't resent them as intruders, but welcome them as friends! Realize that they come to test your faith and to produce in you the quality of endurance. But let the process go on until that endurance is fully developed, and you will find you have become men of mature character with the right sort of independence.[4]

2. Learn who God is. Nothing produces spiritual depth like studying the attributes of God. In that study you may make the rather alarming discovery that you have accepted a caricature rather than the true view of God. You have to question, "How much of my view of God came from Scripture versus from the culture around me (including and especially the clichés of the "Christian" culture)? Mark Twain reportedly said,

The Bible says that God created man in His own image. Now man has returned the favor.

I learned how shallow my concept of God was when I began reading *The Existence and Attributes of God*, written by Stephen Charnock, an English Puritan pastor who lived 1628-1680. Even today this over 300 year-old work is considered the definitive text on God's attributes. Dive into Charnock and you'll be amazed at how little you really know about God and what he's like. For example, writing on God's omnipotence, Charnock wrote:

The power of God is that ability and strength whereby He can bring to pass whatsoever He pleases, whatsoever His infinite wisdom may direct, and whatsoever the infinite purity of His will may resolve . . . As holiness is the beauty of all God's attributes,

*so power is that which gives life and action to all
the perfections of the Divine nature. How vain would
be the eternal counsels, if power did not step in to
execute them. Without power His mercy would be
but feeble pity, His promises an empty sound, His
threatenings a mere scare-crow. God's power is like
Himself: infinite, eternal, incomprehensible; it can
neither be checked, restrained, nor frustrated by
the creature.*[5]

Charnock simply focused his attention on who God is.
I'm sure that changed his life. Replacing the caricatures
and discovering the true nature of God will change your life
as well.

3. Learn your "identity." After we discover who God really
is, we then have to learn who we really are. What is the
believer's "identity" or "position" in Christ? In *The Lion,
the Witch and the Wardrobe*, C. S. Lewis beautifully paints
the picture of position in Christ. Peter, Susan, Edmund and
Lucy are four children who, unbeknownst to them, have been
chosen to be kings and queens of Narnia by its ruler, Aslan
the Lion, a type of Christ. Mr. Beaver tells the children:

*. . . down at Cair Paravel there are four thrones and
it's a saying in Narnia time out of mind that when two
Sons of Adam and two Daughters of Eve sit on those
four thrones, then it will be the end not only of the
White Witch's reign but of her life . . .*[6]

Knowing their prophesied identity, the children proceed
to fight a major battle against the forces of the evil White
Witch, a type of Satan. With their victory at the end of the
story, then they are actually seated on their four thrones:

For then, in the Great Hall of Cair Paravel – that wonderful hall with the ivory roof and the west wall hung with peacocks' feathers and the eastern door which looks towards the sea, in the presence of all their friends and to the sound of trumpets, Aslan solemnly crowned them and led them to the four thrones amid deafening shouts of, "Long Live King Peter! Long Live Queen Susan! Long Live King Edmund! Long Live Queen Lucy! Once a king or queen in Narnia, always a king or queen. Bear it well, Sons of Adam! Bear it well, Daughters of Eve!" said Aslan.[7]

Likewise, as Christians, we have an unrealized identity in Christ. We are:

Chosen children of God (John 1:12)
Adopted into God's family (Eph. 1:5, Rom. 8:15-17)
Joint heirs with Christ (Rom. 8:17)
Members of His body (1 Cor. 12:27)
A redeemed possession of God (Eph. 1:7, Col. 1:13-14)
Righteous in Christ (Rom. 10:4, Phil. 3:9)
A new creation (2 Cor. 5:17)
Citizens of heaven (Phil. 3:20-21)
A temple of God (1 Cor. 3:16)
Dead, buried and resurrected with Christ
(Col. 2:12-14; 3:3)
Seated with Christ in Heaven (Eph. 2:6-7)
Complete in Christ (Col. 2:9-10)
Friends of Christ (John 15:14-15)

Just as the children in the story, we do not know who we really are. Yet, on the highest possible authority, our true identity has been declared. If we truly identify with our position in Christ, we will thirst and be transformed.

4. Recognize the futility of life apart from Christ. Have you come to the point yet of realizing that nothing ultimately matters other than how intimately related you are to Christ? Or, are you still acting like you're going to live forever on earth in your present body and present situation? As illogical as that seems, that describes how most people live their lives – in a state of denial of their earthly temporality. Everything you have can (and will) be taken away at some point – except your relationship with Jesus Christ. So does anything matter more than that relationship? Of course you don't have to lose everything to become seriously thirsty for God, but it often helps, as I've learned from painful personal experience.

So are you desperate? Are you desperate to really know Jesus Christ intimately? Are you thirsty with a thirst only he can satisfy? If so, you're ready for a "face to face" meeting with God.

> *As I pursue my heavenly journey by thy grace let me be known as a man with no aim but that of a burning desire for thee . . .*[8]

Once you've discovered thirst it's time to clear some roadblocks preventing you from truly experiencing the presence of God.

FOR FURTHER THOUGHT & DISCUSSION

1. How would you evaluate your spiritual thirst at the present time?
2. Since becoming a Christian, has your spiritual thirst increased or decreased? Why?

3. What "broken cisterns" have interfered with your spiritual growth?
4. How has affliction increased your thirst?
5. What are you going to do to increase your spiritual thirst?

Chapter Two

Busy Impotency

Christians have never been busier, yet never more spiritually impotent. Why? What is it about the busyness of our contemporary culture that leaves many so empty and powerless? Can we go even further and say that busyness is perhaps the greatest enemy of productivity?

When I was a toddler in the early fifties, my parents were building a home in Illinois. Though I don't remember a lot from that early age, I do remember two different carpenters that worked on that home, as well as my dad talking about their work installing doors. Now understand this was back in the days before pre-hung doors. Every door was individually framed, planed, hinged and fit. It was a process. Floy seemed kind of slow and methodical as he plodded along with his glassy-eyed stare, while Clint was always busy hurrying around with his work. The funny thing was that Floy, the "slow" guy, got more doors hung than Clint, the "fast" guy. When someone in our little town said they wouldn't hire Floy because they thought he was too slow, my dad was quick to tell the story of how he might have *appeared* slow, but actually got more work done. It's a story as old as the tortoise and the hare. The moral of the story is that busyness does not always equal productivity – in fact, it seldom does.

Years later, as a young adult, I was the one building a house. During construction I employed two different excavating contractors and again observed this phenomenon. It was a little different in this case because both guys on their bulldozers seemed "busy," but one got three or four times as much work done as the other. I observed the more productive guy to be very focused and goal-oriented, while the other guy just seemed busy with activity disconnected from the goal.

We falsely correlate busyness with productivity though no relationship exists between them. Busyness is actually the enemy of *true* productivity. Samuel Richardson said:

Those who have least to do are generally the most busy people in the world.[1]

The defeating nature of busyness was summed up by Barbara Ehrenreich this way:

The secret of the truly successful, I believe, is that they learned very early in life how not to be busy.[2]

I believe this also rings true for the spiritually successful: they have avoided the trap of busyness. If busyness dominates your life, expect spiritual impotency to result. The emptiness of busyness, however, can drive us to seek God through

Personal Retreats. At its very core, a Personal Retreat is the antithesis of busyness.

JESUS' EXAMPLE

Was Jesus busy? How did he approach the huge mission before him, the task of redeeming the world from sin? Do we see frantic activity? No. Do we see him sitting down with the disciples and saying:

> *All right you guys - time is short. Pay attention because I don't have time to repeat this. I'm only going to be here for three and half years, so we need to get busy saving the world . . .*

We find no such busyness in the life of Christ in spite of the very limited time he knew he had. Jesus' activity seems almost incidental to his walk with his Father. Jesus never ran anywhere, never rode a horse and never was in a hurry. He walked everywhere he went, yet he had an absolute confidence in getting everything done. In his high priestly prayer he says:

> *I glorified you on earth, **having accomplished the work that you gave me to do.*** (John 17:4)

How many of us "busy" people can say we have accomplished the work God has given us to do? As he gives up his last breath on the cross, he cries out, "It is finished!" What was finished? The work of redemption he came to do. No one ever accomplished more on earth than Jesus Christ in those short three and half years – years absolutely devoid of busyness. I suspect that fact is a stinging rebuke to most of us.

Perhaps the bigger question is why didn't Christ engage in frantic activity? Why wasn't he busy? After all, he knew his days were very limited. He knew he was born to die:

But for this purpose I have come to this hour.
(John 12:27b)

Wouldn't that knowledge push you at least a little toward being busy with your calling?

I believe the answer to that question revolves around one word – focus. Jesus knew what he was here for and what he wasn't here for. Think of all the things Jesus didn't do. Think of all the people he didn't heal, all the miracles he didn't do and all the places he never visited. The many times alone with the Father developed a crystal clear focus on his purpose. Because of those many "face to face" Personal Retreats, as we'll discuss in a later chapter, he knew how to spend his time. Jesus knew that life was primarily about relationships: First the relationship with his Father, and secondly relationships with those he was called to serve. Busyness drives us from those relationships. Likewise, a lack of relationships may drive us to busyness to cover up our emptiness.

We can have that focus Jesus had and escape the impotency of busyness. Dr. Howard Hendricks once said:

Most Christians are busier than God intended them to be.

I remember a story Hendricks shared about visiting a pastor who was a former student of his. The young pastor proudly showed Dr. Hendricks the church bulletin saying, "Look at that, Hendricks. Something going on every night of the week." Hendricks burst his balloon by asking, "And when is someone in your church supposed to cultivate a relationship with his or her family?"

Why do we get wrapped up in all this incessant busyness? I think the answer is simple: **we haven't spent the time alone with God that is necessary to get clear direction**. Because Jesus did spend that time, he never needed to be busy. Pastor Rick Warren notes:

> *Busyness is a great enemy of relationships. We become preoccupied with making a living, doing our work, paying our bills, and accomplishing goals as if these tasks are the point of life. They are not. The point of life is learning to love – God and people. Life minus love equals zero.[3]*

MARY & MARTHA

One of the Bible's most familiar stories of busyness involves two sisters, Mary and Martha:

> *Now as they went on their way, Jesus entered a village. And a woman named Martha welcomed him into her house. And she had a sister called Mary, who sat at the Lord's feet and listened to his teaching. But Martha was distracted with much serving. And she went up to him and said, "Lord, do you not care that my sister has left me to serve alone? Tell her then to help me." But the Lord answered her, "Martha, Martha, you are anxious and troubled about many things, but one thing is necessary. Mary has chosen the good portion, which will not be taken away from her."* (Luke 10:38-42)

Martha was busy; busy to her own detriment. Mary rejected the temptation to busyness by choosing to deepen her relationship with the Lord. I note a certain mutual exclusivity in the passage – either you're busy or you focus on the Lord. Is it not the same today? Can we really be busy doing all the things of life and simultaneously commune with Jesus? I think not. The key word in the above passage is **distracted**. To distract implies a change of focus, a diversion from a superior pursuit to an inferior one. That's exactly what busyness does to us.

I believe we can learn a lot from Jesus' gentle rebuke to Martha. First we see his compassion for us in our anxious state. Note the tenderness and patience in his saying, "Martha, Martha." It is as if Jesus is pained by our unnecessary anxiety. Jesus also gives a great definition of busyness – being troubled by many things. Then the Lord teaches the positive direction by saying, "Only one thing is necessary," namely, what her sister Mary had chosen. That one thing was of course relationship with Jesus. The moral of the story is that you cannot have both. You cannot be wrapped up in busyness and wrapped in a relationship with the living God simultaneously. An intimate relationship with Christ requires undistracted times with him. This need is the motivation for meeting God in a Personal Retreat.

CONFUSING ACTIVITY WITH ACCOMPLISHMENT

Activity and accomplishment are not necessarily related. As with the examples I shared at the beginning of this chapter, you can be very busy, but not accomplish much. If you don't know where you're going, any road will take you there – and the faster you go, the farther you'll end up from the true goal. Obsessive activity produces this same result with people day in and day out.

I recall another story Dr. Howard Hendricks shared in a lecture on leadership principles early in my Christian ministry. It seems there was a missionary working in a very remote jungle village in Brazil that required a three-day canoe trip to reach. Missionary Aviation Fellowship came on the scene and offered to fly the missionary to his village in three hours instead. But the missionary refused their help, preferring to keep paddling his canoe for three days at a time, saying, "This is what God has called me to do." I really doubt that God called the man to canoe paddling. I don't think the Great Commission is to "Go therefore and paddle your canoe!" Paddling the canoe is an activity. Making disciples in a remote jungle would be the desired accomplishment.

That story, though true, seems absurd. Yet don't we all do the same thing when we get caught up in activity, in the routine of whatever we do, rather than staying focused on the goal? Without that time apart with the Lord, we are guaranteed to surrender to the siren song of activity while missing the true goal God desires us to accomplish.

DOING VS. BEING

I wish not so much to do as to be, as I long to be like Jesus.[4]

Spiritual impotency results from **doing** to the exclusion of **being**. Here's the question: When you look at your activity, is the activity "in order to" or "because of?" Activity must flow from identity, not the other way around. Isn't this what we see in the life of Christ? Who he was (identity) determined what he did (activity). The wrong equation is:

What I do → Who I am

The right equation is:

Who I am → What I do

The right activity flows from the right identification.

Test yourself. Do you feel more worthy doing certain activities? Do you really get a sense of identity out of doing the great things? Every occupation and calling has its loftier pursuits. Do I get greater fulfillment out of teaching or preaching or doing a radio or TV program than I do from fixing a leaky pipe under the sink or feeding the horses in the middle of a blizzard? You bet I do. But should I? That's the temptation of activity, especially when one has a lot of exciting things to do. The true grip of that trap, however, is not felt until you have no stunning opportunities for performance.

Do those common activities seem mundane and unimportant? Do you find yourself longing for more successful and glorious activities to lift your spirit? Or is there a way to disentangle yourself from obsession with activity so as to discover the great joy of just **being** who God created you to be, no matter what kind of activity (or lack thereof) you now practice? If you really know who you are, you can find great delight in the present moment, regardless of your present activity.

Personal Retreats teach you "being." After all, how much "doing" can really happen on a retreat? You're alone with no agenda but spending time with God. There is probably (hopefully) no phone. There is no "To Do" list. It may take the first few hours of a Personal Retreat to make the shift from "doing" to "being," but eventually you'll get drawn into the peace of "being" before God. You will enter a world without time and without deadlines. You will discover a world of intimate relationship with God.

The problem if you're wrapped up in busyness is that you won't go on a Personal Retreat. You'll say, "I'm too busy to get away." You don't do a "face to face" with God because you have extra time on your hands, but rather out of an acute sense of need. To truly see your own spiritual impotency will drive you to a Personal Retreat. Emptiness motivates.

Paul described the performance orientation of doing in Romans 7:

I do not understand my own actions. For I do not do what I want, but I do the very thing I hate . . . For I delight in the law of God, in my inner being, but I see in my members another law waging war against the law of my mind and making me captive to the law of sin that dwells in my members. Wretched man that I am! Who will deliver me from this body of death? (Rom. 7:15,22-24)

When you're obsessed with performance, you soon discover that you can never perform well enough. That is the curse of the Law. Even the best, most honorable busyness leaves us unfulfilled.

So how can we really lay hold of this concept, this experience of "being?" I believe that "being" grows out of first recognizing that God has done the "doing." Who we are (our being) results from what he has done (his doing). It is God's doing in creating and redeeming us that gives us our sense of being. Paul soon shifted his focus to the answer to the problem in Romans 8:

There is therefore now no condemnation for those who are in Christ Jesus . . . For God has done [that's God's "doing"] *what the law, weakened by the flesh, could not do. By sending his own Son in the likeness of sinful flesh and for sin, he condemned sin in the flesh, in order that the righteous requirement of the law might be fulfilled in us, who walk not according to the flesh* [that's our "doing"] *but according to the Spirit.* (Rom. 8:1-4)

To live believing what God says about my identity is to escape "doing" and enter into "being."

URGENT VS. IMPORTANT

We are busy with the "urgent," which invariably crowds out the "important." Is life simply an infinite number of squeaky hinges crying out to be oiled? That's what I mean by "urgent." It's all those things that **demand** your immediate action regardless of their true importance or priority. Urgent activities can be everything from a phone that won't stop ringing to administrative busy work to trivial interruptions. The "urgent" always screams for attention – "Do me now!"

By contrast the "important" items in life invariably broadcast at a lower decibel level. The "important" politely requests your time, but doesn't demand it. In fact, sometimes it doesn't vie for your attention at all, but rather waits for you to notice it. It strikes me that the truly "important" activities in life usually involve relationships, while the "urgent" activities either involve "things" or less significant relationships. Watching a live sporting event might be urgent, but it would never be important unless I'm the coach or one of the players. Will I care in the least about that urgent activity a year from now or ten years from now? Compare that to spending that same time with my wife or child. Will that matter a year from now or ten years from now? Absolutely!

The "urgent" demands are omnipresent, but we dare not make them omnipotent lest we become impotent. A wise person will thoughtfully discern between the urgent and important in their life. Focus on the urgent and you end up a slave to neurotic activity. Focus on the important and experience the resulting peace and fulfillment over time. Thoreau wrote:

> *Behind every man's busyness there should be a level of undisturbed serenity and industry, as within the reef encircling a coral isle there is always an expanse of still water, where the depositions are going on which will finally raise it above the surface.*[5]

I know you may be thinking, "How could I ever find time to do a Personal Retreat?" Asking that question is a dead giveaway that you're suffering from busy impotency. I go a little crazy when someone tells me they "don't have time" for something. The last time I checked we all had the same amount of time – 24 hours per day. But we don't all have the same priorities. I've had people marvel that I could take several days away from work just to be alone with God. They have it backwards. How could I have even the slightest chance of functioning, of fulfilling God's purposes for my life without taking off time for that Personal Retreat? Personal Retreats are not a luxury for those fortunate souls with lots of free time on their hands. It is precisely because I am so busy that I must take time for that special meeting with God. Doing otherwise only leads to spiritual impotency.

When we recognize ourselves as human beings, not human doings, we will plug into the source of that being. Why do I take the time to go "face to face" with God? Why do I take the time to eat, to drink and to breathe? It is nothing less than a necessity of life.

PROBLEM OF PRIDE

Why are people "busier than God intended them to be?" Is it anything but ego and pride? To be obsessed with busyness is to think you're indispensable, to think the world will fall apart if you deviate from your frantic pace. By contrast, Personal Retreats reveal your utter insignificance. On a Personal Retreat God gets bigger, and I get smaller. I learn during that time alone that he is really the one in charge. That takes a lot of pressure off. It allows me to enjoy God – imagine that! But what did the famous Westminster Shorter Catechism say in 1646:

> *Question 1: What is the chief end of man?*
> *Answer: Man's chief end is to glorify God, and to* enjoy him forever.

Pride, being the source of Lucifer's fall (Ezek. 28:1-19), comprises the antithesis of Christian maturity. Clinging to busyness in our pride prevents us from knowing God intimately.

POWER OF PERSONAL RETREATS

So what is it exactly that a Personal Retreat does to busy impotency? A meeting with God dissolves the illusions of pride and self-importance. When you get alone with God out in the middle of nowhere, you see life differently. You really begin to experience your own smallness as your awareness of God dramatically increases. Likewise, you shift from doing to being. After all, what else can you do at that remote location? To experience the world going along without you for a day or several days is unbelievably humbling, yet profoundly liberating.

After an initial clearing period on a Personal Retreat, it's just you and God. Instead of being mentally bombarded with all the decisions and responsibilities dogging your life, you actually begin experiencing the presence of God. Your focus turns from knowledge about God to relationship with God. And beyond that, you begin to experience something even greater – friendship with God. That relationship emerges as the only truly important thing. You start seeing things clearly, having been brought back to your true identity as a redeemed child of God.

CONCLUSION

The world desperately strives to squeeze us into its mold (Rom. 12:2, Phillips). But what is this mold the world seeks to conform us to? Is it not a mold of doing, of performance, of ego, of pride? Is it not a mold of busyness disconnected from intimate contact with God? If we are thus squeezed, we are stuck with busy impotency.

The conclusion of the Book of Daniel contains an interesting prophecy of the "end times" that applies to this question:

> *But you, Daniel, shut up the words and seal the book, until the time of the end.* ***Many shall run to and fro***, *and knowledge shall increase.* [Emphasis added] (Dan. 12:4)

I won't speculate on whether we're in the "end times" or not, but that certainly is an appropriate description of most people today – running to and fro. And I must confess – I have been one of those people. We are people who never hear anything from God because we never stop talking long enough. Personal Retreats can break that pattern. For that brief time away they reveal our insignificance and allow us to discover a more intimate relationship with God.

We can escape busyness, yet still be blocked from truly connecting with God. Let's look at another missing ingredient.

FOR FURTHER THOUGHT & DISCUSSION

1. Do you see yourself as a "busy" person?

2. In what ways has your busyness interfered with your spiritual life?

3. How might your life be different if you rejected busyness as a lifestyle?

4. Are you presently confusing activity with accomplishment in your life?

5. Does busyness produce a sense of worth in you? Should it?

6. What "important" activities have you neglected because busyness drove you instead to focus on "urgent" activities?

Chapter Three

Escaping the "Noise"

What is "noise" and how does it interfere with our coming "face to face" with God? Dictionary definitions often amaze me with their depth of meaning. The American Heritage Dictionary provides these various definitions for "noise":

1. *Sound or a sound that is loud, unpleasant, unexpected, or undesired.*

2. *Sound or a sound of any kind.*

3. *Physics: A disturbance, especially a random and persistent disturbance that obscures or reduces the clarity of a signal.*

4. *Computer Science: Irrelevant or meaningless data.*[1]

I really appreciate the physics definition of "noise" being a **persistent disturbance that obscures or reduces the clarity of a signal**, as well as the computer science definition of **irrelevant or meaningless data.** That describes exactly what we're talking about. God's signal is being reduced or obscured by the irrelevant "noise" in our lives.

Equally interesting is the etymology of the word. The English word *noise* comes from the Latin word *nausea*. The original meaning of "seasickness" has expanded to mean a more general discomfort. But you get the idea: noise = gag reflex! Noise, however you define it, is not very desirable. How many parents, "nauseated" by their teenager's music have said, "Turn that noise down!" Physical noise can certainly irritate, but the bigger problem is that all manner and definitions of "noise" interfere with our hearing God.

We best hear God in silence. Larry Crabb writes:

> *Our search for God is therefore an **inward** search. Silence and solitude are essential to discovering His Presence. We must block out the noise of life and become aware of our interior world if we're to find God.*[2]

WHY CAN'T WE HEAR GOD?

It seems that two extremes confront us when it comes to hearing God today. One viewpoint doesn't expect to hear from God, being content to live in a dull, drab, ritualistic faith. The other extreme *demands* that God be continually speaking to each individual Christian. I call the latter view the "God told me" group. Of course, I am usually unconvinced that God has told them anything.

After forty years as a Christian seeing all manner of abuses of God's Word, I am generally leery of those with a "God told me" message, particularly when it contradicts what I sense God is saying to me (and most definitely when it contradicts Scripture). I've known some Christians in this category that were just plain crazy, even to the point of being institutionalized. More commonly it's just a matter of not knowing indigestion from inspiration – both can produce unusual feelings inside your body!

During a particularly long period of suffering, a well-meaning friend sent a "word of knowledge" from some alleged "prophet" she knew. I found it about as inspirational as the average fortune cookie – words that would fit almost anybody in any situation. My immediate thought was, "What a poor substitute this is for the Scripture." Such present day prophetic words (that I have no way of knowing the legitimacy of) pale in comparison to the Psalms, through which the Holy Spirit consistently and tangibly moves me. I quickly realized anew the great superiority of the written Word of God.

There is nothing more profound than the Holy Spirit speaking through the words of Scripture. We definitely should be hearing God, but the emphasis of the Bible is on his speaking through the written Word. Of course God can speak through other means as well – impressions, circumstances, other people and even a donkey once! However, these means are much more subject to misinterpretation and deception. Hearing God is a serious matter, so we must strive to correctly understand this process.

ARE YOU HEARING GOD?

If I ask you, "What has God said to you lately?" What would you say? Would you stammer and stutter, overwhelmed by the question, or would something immediately come to mind? The Word of God is described as being "living and active, sharper than a two-edged sword" (Heb. 4:12), but is God's Word in us similarly "living and active" or perhaps more dead and stagnant? Ask me that question, and I would respond in a heartbeat – primarily because it came from a Personal Retreat I went on last week. But, oh, how much of my Christian life I hadn't a clue as to what God was really saying to me!

But what if I asked a second question: "Would you like to hear from God?" I think most sincere Christians would answer in the affirmative. As mentioned earlier, some get downright obsessed with hearing from God. Plus, I think every Christian has struggled with the question of "How can I know the will of God?" relative to a certain decision before them. So, if we want to hear from God, why can't we?

THE PROBLEM OF "NOISE"

Ever watch a TV reporter at Times Square during New Years or at a political convention demonstration after the nomination of a candidate? They're practically screaming, yet you can't hear them. Why? Noise is the problem. Sometimes you just can't raise the volume enough to overcome the background noise. Though I'm confident God could talk loud enough to be heard over any earthly-generated noise, that just isn't his way.

Suppose you have a very important message to deliver to a friend at a football game where the crowd is screaming wildly after a touchdown. Wouldn't you prefer to take him out of the stands, out of the noise, to speak that message in a calm and understandable way? So would God. He doesn't scream at us to merely become a louder voice amidst the cacophony. Rather, he invites us into the quiet places where we more easily hear him minus all the other distractions. He does what a good friend with a vital message would do.

KINDS OF NOISE

The "noise" that interferes with hearing God comes in many forms:

1. Literal noise – Plain old noise obviously interferes with communication, whether with other people or with God. I don't see too many Christians picking a busy downtown intersection to have their "quiet time." We already know that literal noise defeats communication, so this isn't really an issue.

2. Problems – Problems comprise much of the stuff of life. A problem is:

1. A question to be considered, solved or answered.

2. A situation, matter, or person that presents perplexity or difficulty.

3. A misgiving, objection, or complaint.[3]

What are your problems? Financial, job, marital, children, parents? Though we constantly entertain various problems, such situations create noise in our lives that interferes with hearing God.

3. Worry – Worry is defined as:

1. To feel uneasy or concerned about something; be troubled.

2. To pull or tear at something with or as if with the teeth.

The word "worry" comes from the Middle English *worien*, which meant **to strangle**.[4] What a description of what worry does to us! Pastor Rick Warren says:

When you think about a problem over and over in your mind, that's called worry. When you think about God's Word over and over in your mind, that's meditation. If you know how to worry, you already know how to meditate! You just need to switch your attention from your problems to Bible verses. The more you meditate on God's Word, the less you will have to worry about.[5]

Charles Spurgeon said:

Anxiety does not empty tomorrow of its sorrows, but only empties today of its strength.

Time "face to face" with God in Personal Retreats replaces worry and anxiety over problems with meditation on his answers.

4. Indecision – Decisions result from making up your mind about something. Therefore the difficulty is not so much in that final result, but rather the *indecision* that precedes your conclusion. Should I do this or should I do that? Indecision sucks the life right out of you. Imagine yourself an inflated balloon. Indecision is like sticking a pin in you and letting the air out.

I became a decisive person largely out of reaction to my indecisive father, who subscribed to the "maybe we will, maybe we won't" school of thought. He was indecisive about business, buying a car, buying a home, taking a vacation, spending money – you name it! As a child I watched that indecisiveness, and the fear that motivated it, rob him and those around him of the simple joy of living.

Society pays a high premium to those that know how to make decisions. An executive is simply someone who makes decisions – one who *executes* a plan. Executives of some major corporations receive tens of millions of dollars in annual compensation simply because they know how to make good decisions. I think we can learn from their example. Just as abandoning indecision increases worldly corporate profits, so abandoning indecision for the Christian brings spiritual reward.

Like all the other forms of noise, indecision simply occupies your life making it difficult to hear God. Indecision, like all the other forms of noise, essentially takes you "offline" in what should be a continual dialog with God. It's a great day when you discover that wrong decisions are generally better for you than indecision.

5. Anticipation – To anticipate is to feel or realize beforehand or to look forward to.[6] We usually think that's a good and positive thing, but is it? The more you anticipate about tomorrow, the more noise is in your head today. Jesus said:

> *Therefore do not be anxious about tomorrow, for tomorrow will be anxious for itself. Sufficient for the day is its own trouble. (Matt. 6:34)*

6. Distraction – Distraction is brain clutter. Enough of it will drive you crazy. Again the dictionary definition is most instructive:

1. To cause to turn away from the original focus of attention or interest; divert.

2. To pull in conflicting emotional directions; unsettle.[7]

Literally the word from Latin simply means, "to pull away." We often fall victim to what has been called "the tyranny of the urgent," allowing the things that cry out loudest to us to displace that which is truly important. Thoreau said:

For the most part we allow only outlying and transient circumstances to make our occasions. They are, in fact, the cause of our distraction.[8]

Light emanates from a light bulb as well as from a laser, but the laser is not "distracted." It can cut through steel simply because of this focus. Power is a function of focus. In *The Karate Kid* movies, mentor Mr. Myagi's repeated message to Daniel Laruso is simply "**Focus!**" Focus in karate produces power. Focus spiritually for the Christian produces the experience of the presence of God. A. B. Simpson, founder of the Christian & Missionary Alliance once told friend, William MacArthur:

I am no good unless I can get alone with God.

MacArthur stated:

His practice was to hush his spirit, and literally cease to think, then in the silence of his soul, he listened for the 'still small voice' [of God].[9]

7. Unnecessary Possession – In America, as well as most of the western world, we're buried in "stuff." We seldom distinguish between what we truly need and what we just want (though most of us have an uncanny ability to rationalize our wants into needs). **Materialism curses us because it is noise**. It is simply more things to get in the way of hearing God. Possessions are accompanied by care:

Do not lay up for yourselves treasures on earth, where moth and rust destroy and where thieves break in and steal, but lay up for yourselves treasures in heaven, where neither moth nor rust destroys and where thieves do not break in and steal. For where your treasure is, there your heart will be also. (Matt. 6:19-21)

What you do not have you cannot lose. When it comes to all the "stuff" of life, you must ask yourself, "Do I own it, or does it own me?" It's amazing the way the "things" we really want end up being such a burden to us. Solomon captured this problem in Ecclesiastes:

When goods increase, they increase who eat them, and what advantage has their owner but to see them with his eyes? (Eccles. 4:11)

Though I've never been a boat owner (other than a canoe), I've always been amused by the oft-repeated joke that the two best days in a boat owner's life are the day he bought his boat and the day he sold it. The same could be said for many of the "toys" that can clutter our lives.

Does all this mean we should live the most meager existence possible? Am I saying there's something wrong with a boat or a vacation home or a recreational vehicle or an All Terrain Vehicle? Of course not. But be careful. All these things can be more noise in your life that will interfere with hearing God.

8. Busyness – Our last chapter covered the subject of busyness and how it can divert us from an intimate relationship with God. Busyness is another form of noise. I am firmly convinced that most Christians are far busier than God intends them to be. It seems that if the devil can't destroy your spiritual life by encouraging your *inactivity*, he will try to destroy it with *overactivity*. Either one interferes with intimacy.

TURNING DOWN THE NOISE

Once you recognize the sources of noise in your life, you can begin to turn them down. This, of course, is not instantaneous, but rather a process. It really takes some time. Noise has a residual effect—it just doesn't clear from our heads that easily. Personal Retreats provide an avenue to jump-start the process. It's virtually guaranteed that going on a retreat will clear a lot of the noise, allowing you to begin to hear God.

Get rid of as much "noise" as possible at home and at work. Attacking the sources of noise we've talked about with lifestyle changes can do a lot. But an occasional "face to face" Personal Retreat will greatly enhance the clearing of noise.

PERSONAL RETREATS AND NOISE

Some messages can only be given in a special place away from distraction. At these special times God will tell you to go. Let's take Ezekiel's Personal Retreat as an example.

And the hand of the Lord was on me there, and He said to me, "Get up, go out to the plain, and there I will speak to you." (Ezek. 3:22, NASB)

Commenting on the above verse, Os Hillman writes:

> *When God wants to speak a very important word directly to us without interruption from the noise of our busy lives, he will take us "into the plain." The plain is a place of no distractions and no other persons. It is a place of silence. It can be a place of great need as it often fails to have the normal provisions we are accustomed to. It can be a place we go to voluntarily to seek His face, or we can be moved there without choice by His supernatural ability. More often, it is the latter method that brings us into the plain. In modern times, it often means a separation from our normal activities such as jobs or families. The plain can also be a place where we discover afresh that God's hand has been on us all the time. When we are so busy with life, we sometimes forget that God's hand is still there, gently leading our path. When our lives get so busy that we are not listening or responding to His gentle touch, He must take more aggressive measures to get our attention. Thus, the plain is one of those appointed times of one-on-one communication with our heavenly Father.[10]*

So how do Personal Retreats dissipate the noise? Let's look at some aspects of "noise reduction."

1. Distance – Distance from your surroundings will in and of itself reduce noise. It's as if the familiar items in our lives – home, family, workplace, possessions – manifest a "gravity" that pulls us toward them, that holds us in their orbit. A Personal Retreat launches us like a rocket through the accustomed pull of gravity into another world. Just as with a spacecraft, the farther away the less pull of gravity.

Essentially the retreat narrows your focus from the many things normally in your presence and thoughts to the basics. That's when we best hear God.

2. Unfamiliar Locale – The Personal Retreats in the Bible typically occur in unfamiliar locations, just as in Ezekiel's situation above. **Familiar places breed self-confidence and self-reliance.** They really create in us a kind of pride and sense of control. Unfamiliar places have more of a humbling effect. We more automatically trust God in a strange place where we don't really know where we are or what to expect. **To lose our sense of control is to discover God's sovereign control.** I would even go so far as to say that a place that evokes a little fear produces a deeper spiritual awareness.

3. Solitude – A lot of noise simply results from interaction with other people. Being alone quiets the spirit whether you're on a Personal Retreat or just taking a few minutes by yourself. We're not hermits. The normal pattern of God's life for us involves interaction with people. But periods of solitude are essential to maintaining intimate communications with God; just as they were for Christ during his earthly ministry.

4. Fasting – Since fasting is discussed in detail in Chapter 8, let me just say here that denying the physical appetite opens up the spiritual appetite. I think of fasting as a focusing tool that moves you from meeting your own needs to more exclusively seeking God. I know of nothing that dissipates "noise" quicker than fasting.

DISCOVERING "TRACK 5 MOMENTS"

You know you've cleared the noise away when you experience what I call "Track 5 Moments." A Track 5

Moment occurs when you are overawed with the majesty of God in Creation and driven to worship him.

So where did I get the name "Track 5 Moment?" It comes from Track 5 of the Original Soundtrack of the movie, *Return to Snowy River* composed by Bruce Rowland.[11] It's called "Return to the Mountains," occurring in the movie when the hero and heroine, Jim Craig and Jessica Harrison, ride their horses along a crest of the Snowy Range in Australia to awe-inspiring views below them. It is my favorite scene in my favorite movie, blending the majesty of God's creation with incredibly beautiful and inspiring music. It displays a perfect moment.

I coined the term "Track 5 Moment" a few years ago when I was driving home from a trip to our Central Oregon ranch near sunset. I happened to be listening to the CD of *Return from Snowy River*. Just as I rounded a bend in the road our Three Sisters mountains emerged across a broad, green pasture. It was as if the music was timed for that exact moment. Everything was perfect for that moment – the breathtaking view, the music and the fact that I was privileged to gaze upon that view every day from my home, even as I am doing right now recounting this. My moment duplicated the moment in the movie. Every similar experience of being wowed to worship by God's creation, particularly on many Personal Retreats, has since been called a "Track 5 Moment".

I am hardly the first person to describe this phenomenon. John Muir, writing of the Yosemite Valley, described such a moment when he said:

> *This glorious valley might well be called a church,*
> *for every lover of the great Creator who comes within*
> *the broad overwhelming influences of the place fails*
> *not to worship as they never did before.*[12]

Similarly Gordon Stainforth wrote:

> *It is difficult, when looking at such extravagant inventiveness, to avoid the question: why is so much of nature so unnecessarily beautiful?[13]*

Track 5 Moments are noiseless moments, moments when God's voice shouts from his creation. They are intense, almost Edenic moments when your connection with God is unhindered – when you are "face to face." Personal Retreats invite you to the Track 5 Moment.

CONCLUSION

Our lives are filled with noise, whether it's literal noise or the interference that comes from the various cares of this world. Like the proverbial frog in the pot of water slowly brought to a boil, we are usually unaware of the degree of our distraction. Thus, dissipating noise in our lives can be a shock at first. Your mind can change from being illumined by an unfrosted, glaring bulb to the focus of a laser beam. It may be a new experience, but it's a great experience. As you experience "noise reduction" through Personal Retreats, you will discover a whole new spiritual world with a depth previously unknown to you.

Yet this "noise reduction experience is not new. The saints of old knew the problem and solution well, as we will see in the Bible beginning with Abraham.

FOR FURTHER THOUGHT & DISCUSSION

1. Has "noise" as described in this chapter interfered with your knowing God in a deeper way? How?

2. Do you "hear" God speaking to you on a regular basis? If not, what do you think is the reason?

3. Which sources of "noise" trouble you the most – literal noise, problems, worry, indecision, anticipation, distraction, unnecessary possession, or busyness? Describe.

4. Have you ever experienced the greater presence of God in a distant, unfamiliar place?

5. Describe what this chapter called a "Track 5 Moment" in your life.

Face to Face

Chapter Four

Since Abraham

If Personal Retreats are important and legitimate, there must be biblical examples. The "face to face" encounters I call a "Personal Retreat" occur throughout the Bible. . . ever since Abraham. Instances of "getting alone" with God for direction and refreshment provide important examples for us centuries later. Speaking of the Israelites wandering in the wilderness, the Apostle Paul wrote:

Now these things happened to them as an example, but they were written down for our instruction, on whom the end of the ages has come. (1 Cor. 10:11)

The events of the Old Testament stand ready to teach us in the faith. The retreats of different Old Testament characters show us not only the importance, but moreover the varying purposes for Personal Retreats.

ABRAHAM – RESPONSIVENESS

And if you are Christ's, then you are Abraham's offspring, heirs according to the promise.
(Gal. 3:29)

Abraham, the New Testament tells us, is the father of all who believe (Rom. 4:11,16). Surely if this concept of Personal Retreats is legitimate and important, we will find them in the life of Abraham.

Scripture reveals numerous instances of God speaking to Abraham. We don't always know where these encounters took place, whether just during his daily routine or away at a remote place. However, we do know of one time for sure that God took Abraham away to a special place for one of the Bible's most gripping "face to face" encounters – the sacrifice of Isaac.

This most famous story about Abraham revolved around a Personal Retreat. We read in Genesis 22:1-5:

After these things God tested Abraham and said to him, "Abraham!" And he said, "Here am I." He said, "Take your son, your only son Isaac, whom you love, and go to the land of Moriah, and offer him there as a burnt offering on one of the mountains of which I shall tell you." So Abraham rose early in the morning, saddled his donkey, and took two of his young men with him, and his son Isaac. And he cut the wood for the burnt offering and arose and went to the place of which God had told him. On the third day Abraham lifted up his eyes and saw the place from afar. Then Abraham said to his young men, "Stay here with the donkey; I and the boy will go over there and worship and come again to you."

What a story of testing! What a story of proving the **responsiveness** of a man to God! I find myself choking up just rereading this passage as I write this chapter. It's important to note at the outset that God initiates this Personal Retreat. God tells Abraham to go to the mountains to a place to be revealed. The passage tells us the place was three days journey – definitely away from Abraham's usual residence and environment.

The focus of this event was worship, which I find very instructive to how we should orient our retreats. Note that he doesn't say to his servants, "I'm going to go over yonder and sacrifice Isaac" (even though that's what God told him to do). Rather he says, "We're going over there *to worship* **and we're coming back** – both of us." Is it any wonder a man with that kind of faith is called "the father of all who believe?" Any Personal Retreat must have this same worship focus no matter what other specific objectives might be involved.

Abraham shows unflinching faith in raising the knife, a test I'm sure all of us tremble at the mere thought of. The New Testament tells us why in Hebrews 11:17-19:

> *By faith Abraham, when he was tested, offered up Isaac, and he who had received the promises was in the act of offering up his only son, of whom it was said, "Through Isaac shall your offspring be named." He considered that God was able even to raise him from the dead, from which, figuratively speaking, he did receive him back."*

God had already told Abraham that a multitude of descendants would come through his son, Isaac. He so believed God that the only possible conclusion in the situation was that God would raise him from the dead. That's the kind of perspective that only years of developing an intimate relationship with God can produce.

This isn't just a great story of one man's faith expressed on a Personal Retreat, but is a type of our redemption. The father sacrifices the son. The male sheep is provided as a substitute. Isaac came from the dead in the first place – from the reproductive deadness of Abraham and Sarah. Likewise, we were spiritually dead. The site of the sacrifice of Isaac on Mt. Moriah later became the location of the Altar of Sacrifice in Solomon's Temple.

So why did God take Abraham three days away? In addition to the parallel with the resurrection of Christ and taking him to the future temple sacrifice site, I believe it also offers a pattern for a Personal Retreat. God must take us away from the familiar when there's a special message to deliver. He needed Abraham's undivided attention and thus devised a private, intimate journey for him. God's purposes for this testing would have never worked at home with Sarah around – "God told you to do what with my son? Over my dead body you're going to sacrifice him!" I don't think that would have worked! That was an additional battle Abraham didn't need to fight – he needed to be alone with God and so do we for the tests he has for us. And remember, you and I are here today as believers in Jesus Christ because of Abraham's Personal Retreat.

> *May the Spirit of God assist you to leave the mists of fear, the fevers of anxiety, and all the ills that gather in this valley of earth and to ascend the mountains of anticipated joy and blessing . . . May our souls, like Abraham, attain the mountaintop and there commune with the Most High.* (Charles Spurgeon)[1]

JACOB — REPENTANCE

The life of Jacob provides a great testimony to the grace of God. From eternity God unconditionally loved Jacob (Rom. 9:13), yet he was a liar and cheat at heart. He defrauded his brother, Esau, of his birthright, and he defrauded his father-in-law, Laban, of the best of his herd (although we're typically unsympathetic to Laban, who was an even worse crook than Jacob).

Jacob's first encounter with God occurs when he flees Isaac and Rebekah's home and the ire of his now defrauded brother, Esau. Though I don't particularly see this encounter as a Personal Retreat, it does set the stage for a later retreat. In Genesis 28:10-22 we read the story of Jacob's dream. Taking a stone for a pillow, he dreams of a ladder to heaven with angels ascending and descending on it. Here Jacob's destiny is revealed:

> *I am the Lord, the God of Abraham your father and the God of Isaac. The land on which you lie I will give to you and to your offspring. Your offspring shall be like the dust of the earth and you shall spread abroad to the west and to the east and to the north and to the south, and in you and your offspring shall all the families of the earth be blessed.* (Gen. 28:13b-14)

Though Jacob learns his destiny in this divine encounter, he isn't really ready for the fulfillment of the vision. He is still Jacob – the supplanter, as his subsequent twenty-year relationship with Laban shows.

Leaving Laban it is finally time for Jacob to return home. But in the sovereignty of God, Jacob is cornered and driven to a "face to face" Personal Retreat for **repentance**. It climaxes one dark, lonely night in the desert:

The same night he arose and took his two wives, his two female servants, and his eleven children, and crossed the ford of the Jabbok. He took them and sent them across the stream, and everything else that he had. And Jacob was left alone. And a man wrestled with him until the breaking of the day. When the man saw that he did not prevail against Jacob, he touched his hip socket, and Jacob's hip was put out of joint as he wrestled with him. Then he said, "Let me go, for the day has broken." But Jacob said, "I will not let you go unless you bless me." And he said to him, "What is your name?" And he said "Jacob." Then he said, "Your name shall no longer be called Jacob, but Israel, for you have striven with God and with men and have prevailed." (Gen. 32:22-28)

Why did Jacob send everyone else across the stream and remain alone? Was not God bringing the deceiver to the end of himself? Did Jacob not sense that he had to be alone with God? Jacob knew his identity and destiny in part as a son of Isaac and grandson of Abraham. However, he lacked the humility necessary to fulfill God's purpose for his life. Jacob had to be broken by God. He had to exhaust all his human strength in this angelic battle for his soul, just as we typically have to exhaust our strength to discover and receive the grace of God. We best face God and ourselves when alone, for we have to be alone to wrestle with God.

So what did Jacob's Personal Retreat accomplish? Jacob (meaning "one who supplants") became Israel (meaning "he who strives with God"). Though already promised to Abraham and Isaac, the nation of Israel was born that dark night in the desert. God's plan of redemption was set in motion, through which the Scriptures and the Messiah would come. The pattern continues through the Bible even up to our day, in that when God wants to do something special through someone, he usually takes them on a Personal Retreat.

Have you resisted God's call to go out and be alone with him? Is there a great thing God would do in and through your life that awaits a time alone wrestling with him? Let your desperation for God's blessing in your life drive you to those special times alone in his presence.

MOSES – REVELATION

Like Abraham, God regularly spoke to Moses on many occasions recorded in the Bible beginning with the burning bush. But it is his encounter with God on Mt. Sinai that most represents the concept of a Personal Retreat – a retreat for **revelation** of God. Again we see the classic template: (1) He was called by God to go to a special place for a private meeting; (2) He was alone, separated from his people; (3) A significant event was to occur – receiving God's Law; (4) It was an intensely powerful experience. We read in Exodus 19:16-20:

> *On the morning of the third day there were thunders and lightnings and a thick cloud on the mountain and a very loud trumpet blast, so that all the people in the camp trembled. Then Moses brought the people out of the camp to meet God, and they took their stand at the foot of the mountain. Now Mount Sinai was wrapped in smoke because the Lord had descended on it in fire. The smoke of it went up like the smoke of a kiln, and the whole mountain trembled greatly. And as the sound of the trumpet grew louder and louder,*

Moses spoke, and God answered him in thunder. The Lord came down on Mount Sinai, to the top of the mountain. **And the Lord called Moses to the top of the mountain, and Moses went up.**

Though God had already been speaking to Moses, for the special occasion of giving the Law, he called him (with great fanfare) to go alone to the top of the mountain. It was a Personal Retreat, albeit perhaps the most dramatic one ever recorded in Scripture. The most powerful statement of right and wrong in all of human history resulted from that encounter with God.

But let's not just look at the "Mt. Sinai Personal Retreat" in terms of what God did for mankind there. What about Moses himself? What did this Personal Retreat and all his other encounters with God do for him? What kind of a man did he become? Like Abraham the pagan idolater and Jacob the supplanter, Moses was flawed. He was raised in the pagan Egyptian culture as royalty. He was proud and arrogant. When he first grasped his calling to deliver Israel, he plowed ahead in his own strength killing and burying the Egyptian that was oppressing a fellow Israelite. In fear he fled to the wilderness of Midian for forty years where, alone in the desert, he truly comes into genuine relationship with God. We read of the ultimate result of these encounters with God in his life:

Now the man Moses was very meek, more than all people who were on the face of the earth.
(Num. 12:3)

This is a description of one who has met with God. I remember one of my professors, commenting on this passage, who defined meek as "having great zeal for God, but no selfish ambition." We read an even more stunning description of the transformed life of Moses in Deuteronomy 34:10:

> *And there has not arisen a prophet since in Israel like Moses, whom the Lord knew face to face . . .*

Imagine what it would be to literally know God face to face! Would you desire to know God as Moses did? Though we don't see God literally "face to face," we most definitely can metaphorically come "face to face" experiencing his presence. Moses leads us by example into Personal Retreats.

ELIJAH – RESTORATION

My favorite Old Testament story of a Personal Retreat is that of Elijah. I find great comfort in seeing how God encountered and restored the despondent prophet. Elijah's encounter with God, unlike those of Abraham, Jacob and Moses, was not for doing some great thing like receiving the Covenant or the Law. Rather it was for Elijah's own personal **restoration**. This Personal Retreat was the remedy for the physically, emotionally and spiritually exhausted prophet.

Let's review the story of Elijah from 1 Kings 18 and 19. Defeating the prophets of Baal on Mt. Carmel undoubtedly ranks as the high point of Elijah's life and ministry (1 Kings 18:20-39). He actually saw God send fire out of the sky to consume his offering in direct answer to his prayer. He then slaughtered 450 prophets of Baal and 400 prophets of Asherah, bringing the righteous judgment of God to the vile idolaters who had led God's people astray from the true faith (1 Kings 18:40). What kind of a man would be capable of handling such an intense challenge without flinching? To put it bluntly, Elijah had guts.

After this defeat of the satanic religion of his day, he prophesies rain after the long drought God had brought as a judgment to the Baal-worshipping Israelites. This began with repeated prayer from atop Mt. Carmel (1 Kings 18:42-45). Elijah, due to his intimacy with God, knew he was sending rain, though there wasn't a cloud in the sky. He continues to pray and seven times sent his servant to look for the rain cloud, which finally appears. What faith! I would have given up and quit praying long before he did.

But then it really gets exciting as Elijah, after sending the message to Ahab of the coming deluge, supernaturally outruns Ahab's chariot to Jezreel in the great rainstorm that has commenced. What a fearless and faithful man he was!

But then one woman threatens his life and he falls apart:

Ahab told Jezebel all that Elijah had done, and how he had killed all the prophets with the sword. Then Jezebel sent a messenger to Elijah, saying, "So may the gods do to me and more also, if I do not make your life as the life of one of them by this time tomorrow." Then he was afraid, and he arose and ran for his life and came to Beersheba, which belongs to Judah, and left his servant there. (1 Kings 19:1-3)

Commenting on this passage Dr. Howard Hendricks writes:

Single-handedly he took on 850 prophets, but one woman said, "I'll get you," and he ran. "Lord, I've had it. I'm turning in my prophet's badge."[2]

Elijah journeys 120 miles from the beautiful mountaintop of Carmel to the flat desert of Beersheba – literally and figuratively. After his greatest victory, he fell into defeat and despondency. What a great time to go on a Personal Retreat. And so he did. Elijah's Personal Retreat begins as he goes a day's journey into the wilderness. He continues the pattern of going away and getting alone with God. Oh, how I identify at this point! When I have suffered a great attack or a crushing defeat, I most desire to just go away to a remote place and be alone with God. It reminds me of the anonymous poem "Sir Andrew:"

"I am not dead," Sir Andrew cried,
"I am hurt, but not slain.
I'll just lie here and bleed awhile,
And then I'll rise and fight again."

Believe it or not, there are times when we need to "lie here and bleed awhile" before we "rise and fight again." We require times of restoration from the battles of life.

In his deep depression Elijah begs for God to take his life. He has hit bottom having lost all hope. That, of course, was one prayer God did not answer. Isn't it great that God gives us what we need and not what we want? God implemented a plan of restoration for Elijah. It began with something simple – **sleep**.

Elijah has been writing checks his body can't cash. He is physically exhausted from his ceaseless activity. It's the same with us today. I can tell you, as a health practitioner, that if you don't get enough sleep, you will be depressed – you will lose the joy of your salvation. Frankly, most people I see professionally are exhausted. As physical exhaustion increases, spiritual intimacy with God decreases. How often

I have begun a Personal Retreat with sleeping. We get so wrapped up in our own significance that we assume the world's going to fall apart if we aren't busy. God teaches us both his all-sufficient grace and our utter insignificance with sleep. We're humans, not angels. We have human bodies, not angelic ones. Of our needs for physical restoration, sleep is one of the most basic. Howard Hendricks tells an instructive story relative to this point:

> I got off a plane for a week of meetings in a church pastored by one of our graduates. This man's wife hurriedly took me off on the side while he went to get my bags, and she said, "Professor Hendricks, while you're here, I wonder if you can help my husband. He is constantly active. He spends no time in rest. He is not recouping his strength and his energies, as you often exhorted us to do. I'm afraid he's going to crack up. He's averaging about four to five hours of sleep a night." A few days went by and we were driving along in the car, and I said to him, "How come you don't smoke?" "How come I don't smoke?" "Yes, I've been here all week and I noticed you don't smoke." He said, "Professor Hendricks, my body is the temple of the Holy Spirit." I said, "That's wonderful, that's very good thinking. Is that also the reason you are prostituting your body with four to five hours of sleep a night?"[3]

How easily we miss the obvious!

After some sleep Elijah is awakened and fed by an angel and then goes back to sleep. He still needed more rest. A second time the angel awakens and feeds him for the long journey he is being sent on (1 Kings 19:5-6). By the way, this was the first "angel food cake," though it bore no resemblance to the white sugar, white flour abomination going by that name today. This was supernatural food that enabled Elijah to travel for forty days without additional food on a 200-mile journey to Mt. Horeb, otherwise known as Mt. Sinai.

Why Mt. Sinai? Why does God direct him on such a long trip for his next "face to face?" This is a special place. Elijah is taken to the same place Moses met with God and received the Law. If you wanted to meet with God, what better place to go to than Mt. Sinai! He goes back to the nation's origins.

Sometimes it's appropriate for us to do the same. Is there a special place in your spiritual history? Perhaps it would be the place where you surrendered your life to Christ. Just as the Israelites erected monuments like the stones at the Jordan River crossing to remember what God had done in the past, so we occasionally need to return to our spiritual roots. This is especially true in times of fear and doubt and disillusionment.

At Sinai, Elijah enters a cave – perhaps the ultimate of getting alone and isolated. It is there that God speaks to him. A conversation ensues with God asking, "What are you doing here, Elijah?" The prophet proceeds to extol his own righteousness and bemoan the wickedness of the culture around him – something I'm sure neither you nor I have ever done. His false conclusion – I'm the only true believer left! Though we tend to look at this story in terms of God ministering to the nation, at the heart of the story is God restoring just one man, Elijah. As God moves Elijah through the restoration process we now see a man clinging to a kernel of pride. Elijah is likewise discovering who he really is, and more importantly, who God really is.

God doesn't immediately correct Elijah's false assessment, but rather demonstrates the greatness of his presence. The Lord puts on a little "show" for the prophet. First the wind tears apart the mountains and rocks followed by an earthquake and fire (1 Kings 19:11-12). But the passage says that the Lord was not in the wind or the earthquake or the fire. Then comes a low whisper that Elijah recognizes as the voice of God, who again asks, "What are your doing here, Elijah?"

This is a profound lesson for Personal Retreats. To truly encounter God, Elijah had to see the majesty and power of God, as well as hear his still, small voice. Our number one objective for a Personal Retreat should be exactly the same – **to behold his majesty and hear his voice.** That will put all of our concerns in proper perspective. When we, like Elijah, look at our life or our world and see ungodly chaos, God directs not into a program to change the world, but to an opening of our eyes to behold his sovereign majesty.

The next step in Elijah's restoration is work – God gives him a job to do. There's nothing worse than an unemployed prophet. It is ironic that though we may want to escape our work to lie on that beach in Hawaii, that satisfaction is short-lived. I know, because I've done just that – for thirty minutes or so, anyway! We were created to do the works of God, and we get kind of bored with inactivity. Being occupied with God's will is healing. Note the balance, though: There is a time for work and a time for reflection and rest, as God himself demonstrated at the creation with the Sabbath.

Finally, after all this, God gently rebukes Elijah's "I only am left" lament by telling him there are 7000 true believers that have not bowed to Baal. What do we learn from this? This tells me that an encounter with God ultimately gives the answer, but that God gives that answer at the right time. God is more concerned with restoring and healing me, with conforming me to the image of Christ, than merely answering my questions.

PAUL – RELATIONSHIP

Biblical examples of Personal Retreats do not end with the Old Testament patriarchs and prophets. Before looking at Christ's extensive usage of Personal Retreats, I want to examine the extensive retreat of the Apostle Paul in which he established his **relationship** with Christ.

While Paul's Damascus Road conversion is one of the New Testament's most memorable stories, most people are not so familiar with what happened next. We read in Acts 9:19-25 that, immediately after his baptism, Paul spent time with the Christians in Damascus and began proclaiming Jesus as the Messiah in the local synagogues. It's not hard to imagine the zeal of this new convert who had just personally encountered the resurrected Christ. All the energy he previously exerted in persecuting Christians was now directed to proclaiming Christ.

Paul's early evangelistic ministry is short-lived, however, being interrupted by the Jews' plot to kill him. Thanks to the Damascus believers lowering him in a basket through a hole in the city wall during the dark of night, his life is spared. Though the Book of Acts next places Paul in Jerusalem (Acts 9:26f), a considerable period of time has elapsed, as described by Paul in the Epistle to the Galatians:

But when he who had set me apart before I was born, and who called me by his grace, was pleased to reveal his son to me, in order that I might preach him among the Gentiles, I did not immediately consult with anyone; nor did I go up to Jerusalem to those who were apostles before me, but I went away into Arabia, and returned again to Damascus. Then after three years I went up to Jerusalem to visit Cephas and remained with him fifteen days. (Gal. 1:15-18)

Though many say that Paul spent three years in Arabia, the passage simply says that three years elapsed between his conversion and his trip to Jerusalem. I think it is reasonable, however, to assume that Paul spent most of that three-year time interval in Arabia on a Personal Retreat. The Wycliffe Bible Commentary notes:

The Apostle mentions Arabia not as a place for preaching, because, even though preaching was in view in the call, it is not the subject under consideration at this point. Paul is discussing the source of his Gospel. He mentions Arabia to contrast with Jerusalem. No apostle was to be found there. No one was there who could inform him about the Lord and His saving work. It is probable that the new convert journeyed to Arabia to be alone with God, to think through the implications of the gospel. There is no need to suppose that every aspect of the truth was flashed into his mind at the time of his conversion.[4]

Paul's story reminds me of Moses, whose zeal as a new "convert" to God's cause likewise incited the wrath of the powers that be. As a result of the immature expression of his newly found faith, Moses had to spend forty years in the desert being humbled and prepared for his eventual service. I find it interesting that Moses' Personal Retreat receiving the Law of God was in what was then called Arabia (Gal. 4:25). Paul likewise goes to Arabia to learn the Grace of God. As with Moses, we know comparatively little of the content of Paul's time in Arabia. But we can make some educated speculations.

Paul did not walk and talk with Jesus during the three years of Lord's earthly ministry. Rather Paul spent a similar amount of time being taught by Christ in the desert of Arabia. As the other apostles came to know Christ during his incarnate humiliation, Paul built his relationship during Christ's ascended glorification. The other apostles had three years together with Jesus, while Paul had three years alone with Jesus. What a Personal Retreat that must have been! Imagine the extent of teaching Christ revealed to Paul to enable him to write the majority of the New Testament Epistles. Paul had so much to learn to go from being the "Pharisee of Pharisees" to the champion of God's sovereign grace. Just as God taught the Law to Moses during a forty day Personal Retreat on Sinai, so God taught grace to Paul during his years in Arabia.

What about Paul's vision of being caught up to the third heaven? Very possibly this occurred during his Arabian Personal Retreat. We read of the encounter in 2 Corinthians:

> *I know a man in Christ who fourteen years ago was caught up to the third heaven – whether in the body or out of the body I do not know, God knows. And I know that this man was caught up into paradise – whether in the body or out of the body I do not know, God knows – and he heard things that cannot be told, which man may not utter.* (2 Cor. 12:2-4)

Given that the second Corinthian letter was written around 54 AD, fourteen years earlier would place the described event toward the close of Paul's time in Arabia. Though we can't absolutely establish this dramatic encounter with God during the retreat in Arabia, it does seem somewhat likely. Such revelations of God normally come in times of isolation.

Paul's Personal Retreat in Arabia follows the pattern noted with the earlier biblical figures. God revealed the distinctive theology of Christianity to Paul during an extended time alone, just as he revealed the theology of Judaism to Moses through a similar time away. When God has a special revelation to give or a special work to do, he usually uses a Personal Retreat.

CONCLUSION

So what do all these biblical examples fundamentally teach us? Doesn't it ultimately come down to the simple fact that God desires an intimate relationship with us – that he desires to meet us "face to face?" For such a relationship we were created. The development of that relationship requires periodic special times away with him. Just as some of history's most significant events resulted from such times, so does God even today reveal his purposes for our lives. Your Personal Retreats will probably not result in receiving something like the Abrahamic Covenant or the Mosaic Law or the theology of the New Testament, but they will be just as significant for fulfilling God's unique purpose for your life. Personal Retreats today, just as with the biblical heroes of the faith, often mark major turning points in your life. However, the ultimate objective remains simply to come to know God more deeply and completely.

As profound as the Personal Retreats of these biblical characters, they pale in significance to the ultimate example found in our next subject – Jesus Christ himself.

FOR FURTHER THOUGHT & DISCUSSION

1. Why did God direct Abraham to such a remote location to reveal himself?

2. Which of these biblical examples of "face to face" encounters with God do you most identify with – Abraham, Jacob, Moses, Elijah or Paul? Why?

3. What do all the "face to face" encounters described in this chapter have in common?

4. How could Elijah go from spiritual victory to such despondency in such a short time?

5. How do you think Paul's Personal Retreat in Arabia helped transform him into the Apostle we read of in the Bible?

Face to Face

Chapter Five

Jesus: "Come Apart" (or come apart)

No one utilized Personal Retreats like Jesus Christ. They occur from the beginning to the end of his earthly ministry. Far too often, conservative, Bible-believing Christians miss the perfect humanity of Christ in our desire to defend his perfect divinity. He is both. To understand and appreciate the significance of Jesus' usage of Personal Retreats, we must first understand the Lord's humanity. The incarnate Son, as the second Adam without sin, demonstrates life as God intended . . . and that includes Personal Retreats.

One passage in Scripture especially instructs us in the significance of Christ's humanity. Theologians call it the "kenosis" passage, after the Greek word for "emptying" used in the text:

Have this attitude in yourselves which was also in Christ Jesus, who, although He existed in the form of God, did not regard equality with God a thing to be grasped, but emptied Himself, taking the form of a bond-servant, and being made in the likeness of men. And being found in appearance as a man, He humbled Himself by becoming obedient to the point of death, even death on a cross. (Phil. 2:5-8, NAS)

Though fully God, He laid aside his divine attributes to come and be a man to fulfill God's plan of redemption. In his earthly life Christ is not omniscient, omnipotent, or omnipresent, though these and other attributes of the Godhead are manifested in him at certain times in the Gospels. It is in union with the Father and Spirit that he does the works of God. Though never ceasing to be fully God during his earthly life, Christ voluntarily limited himself to model true humanity for us.

We miss a lot when we fail to see the perfect humanity of Christ along with his perfect divinity. Seeing his divinity will drive us to worship, but seeing also his humanity empowers us to live a life patterned from God's ideal. Christ's humanity was like our own, except he had no sin nature. Christ was not a son of Adam; he was the Son of God. Due to his miraculous conception, he had no human father to pass on the adamic nature. Jesus Christ on earth, though fully God, is man as God originally intended. R. C. Sproul writes:

Christ's humanity was like ours. He became a man "for our sakes." He entered into our situation to act as our Redeemer.[1]

The Church has struggled considerably over the centuries in comprehending the divine and human nature of Christ. Again, Sproul notes:

> *That God the Son took upon Himself a real human nature is a crucial doctrine of historic Christianity. The great ecumenical Council of Chalcedon in A.D. 451 affirmed that Jesus is truly man and truly God and that the two natures of Christ are so united as to be without mixture, confusion, separation, or division, each nature retaining its own attributes.*[2]

The Council of Chalcedon stated:

Following, then, the holy fathers, we unite in teaching all men to confess the one

and only Son, our Lord Jesus Christ. This selfsame one is perfect both in deity

and in humanness; this selfsame one is also actually God and actually man, with

a rational soul [meaning a human soul] *and a body. He is of the same reality as*

God as far as his deity is concerned and of the same reality as we ourselves as far

as his humanness is concerned; thus like us in all respects, sin only excepted.

Before time began he was begotten of the Father, in respect of his deity, and now

in these "last days," for us and behalf of our salvation, this selfsame one was born of Mary the virgin, who is God-bearer in respect of his humanness.

So what's the point of this theological discussion? Simply this: If Jesus Christ as perfect man needed Personal Retreats, then so do we. If we properly understand the "kenosis" we will not look on the way Christ lived on earth as unique to him (and irrelevant to us), but as an example for us. Personal Retreats were a necessary and regular part of the life of Christ. He perfectly exemplifies the purpose and practice of spending isolated time alone with God. As we saw with other biblical figures, Christ's retreats involved different motivations and purposes. Let's look at some of Jesus' Personal Retreats.

THE TEMPTATION

True to pattern Jesus began his ministry with a Personal Retreat in the desert.

Jesus went immediately from initiation into his earthly ministry at baptism to a time of testing:

Then Jesus was led up by the Spirit into the wilderness to be tempted by the devil. (Matt. 4:1)

Nothing accidental here – Christ was **led** by the Holy Spirit to be tempted. Herein we see another purpose for Personal Retreats – testing.

This is a classic Personal Retreat fitting the biblical pattern: It was Spirit-led. He was alone in a remote place. Visiting this area gives one a true appreciation for the story. The "wilderness" refers to the Judean desert between Jerusalem and Jericho. I remember vividly gazing up on these barren mountains from Jericho to the monastery supposedly at the site of the temptation. This area is definitely remote.

This Personal Retreat also involved fasting:

*And after fasting forty days and forty nights, he was
hungry.* (Matt. 4:2)

Later, I have devoted a full chapter to fasting on Personal
Retreats. Though not all retreats require fasting, in some
instances it is very appropriate. In this instance it was
essential to the outcome.

So what were the results of Christ's first recorded
Personal Retreat? The Devil was defeated, plus Christ was
vindicated and confirmed for his ministry. I believe we also
see the adequacy of the Spirit indwelling the man Jesus. We
can count on that same adequacy when we are tempted.

HABITUAL PRACTICE

Personal Retreats were the normal, habitual practice of
Christ. Undoubtedly, only a few are actually recorded for us
in Scripture:

*But Jesus Himself continued His habit of retiring to
lonely spots and praying.* (Luke 5:16; Williams)[3]

What I call "Personal Retreats" were just part of Jesus'
routine. Getting "face to face" with God out on some lonely
mountain or desert was just automatic behavior for him.
This typically happened before events of major significance
or after times of strenuous, draining ministry.

CHOOSING THE TWELVE

Few things Jesus did were more important than choosing
the twelve apostles. The future of the Church and its message,
humanly speaking, depended on choosing the right ones.
Jesus approached this task like everything depended on it
(because it did):

In these days he went out to the mountain to pray, and all night he continued in prayer to God. And when day came, he called his disciples and chose from them twelve, whom he named apostles.
(Luke 6:12-13)

This was a Personal Retreat of **decision**. Faced with a major decision, Jesus retreats to the mountain to pray all night. He had to clearly discern the Father's will for determining the men whose testimony would build the Church. Commenting on this passage, Charles Spurgeon said:

If ever anyone could have lived without prayer, it would have been our spotless and perfect Lord. Yet no one prayed as much as He. Such was His love for fellowship with His Father . . . The time He chose was admirable. It was the hour of silence when the crowd would not disturb Him. It was the time of rest when all but Jesus had ceased laboring. While others slumbered through their problems, Jesus refreshed Himself in prayer. The place was well selected. He was alone. No one would intrude or observe. He was free from Pharisaic ostentation and vulgar [meaning "common"] interruptions. Those dark and silent hills were a proper chapel for the Son of God. Heaven and earth in midnight stillness heard the groans and sighs of the mysterious Being in whom both worlds were blended. His continual pleading is remarkable. The long night watches were not too long. The cold wind did not chill His devotions. The grim darkness did not darken His faith. The loneliness did not check His supplications. The timing of this prayer is notable. It was after His enemies had been enraged that prayer

*was His refuge and comfort. It was before He sent
out the twelve apostles that prayer was the gate of
His enterprise, the herald of His new work. Learn
from Jesus and resort to special prayer when you are
going through a difficult trial or contemplating a new
endeavor for the Master's glory.[4]*

Many times in my life, burdened with major decisions,
God has led me to a Personal Retreat. Though I've prayed
a lot during these times, much of my time was spent just
clearing my head and listening. It is wonderful to watch the
most complicated decisions simplify as one is alone in a
remote place for a couple of days. I use Personal Retreats for
this purpose more than any other. Faced with an important
decision your time could not be better spent than on a
Personal Retreat.

BETHSAIDA

What I call the Bethsaida Personal Retreat involved two
purposes: (1) Mourning the execution of John the Baptist,
and (2) Debriefing and recharging after intense ministry. In
Matthew 14:13 we read that, after hearing of John's death,
Jesus went to a lonely place by himself. Luke's account adds
that he took the disciples with him, and they went to Bethsaida,
a fishing community on the northeast side of the Sea of Galilee
(Luke 9:10). The account in Matthew emphasizes John's death
as the reason for this Personal Retreat:

And his disciples [John the Baptist's disciples] *came
and took the body and buried it, and they went and
told Jesus. Now when Jesus heard this, he withdrew
from there in a boat to a desolate place by himself.*
(Matt. 14:12-13a)

Again we see the perfect humanity of the Lord. John the Baptist was probably a cousin of Jesus. The angel, Gabriel, identifies John's mother, Elizabeth, as a relative of the Virgin Mary. Though the King James Version translates the Greek word *sungenos* as "cousin," it more literally simply means a relative, so we don't know the exact relationship. If, during her pregnancy with Jesus, Mary went to visit Elizabeth, I think we can assume that John and Jesus probably knew each other growing up. John prepared the way for Jesus' ministry as the forerunner prophesied in Isaiah (Matt. 3:3). The birth of Jesus' ministry was the death of John's ministry with the latter's imprisonment following soon after. Jesus said of John:

> *Truly I say to you, among those born of women there has arisen no one greater than John the Baptist.* (Matt. 11:11a)

Given their relationship it is no stretch to assume that Jesus was deeply hurt by the news of John's execution. This was no time for public ministry. He just wanted to be alone with the disciples. He needed to mourn. Thus, it was in part a Personal Retreat of **mourning**.

But there's more to this retreat than mourning. The account in Mark emphasizes the debriefing and recharging as the other purpose for this Personal Retreat. We **"come apart"** or we **come apart**:

> *And he said unto them, **Come ye yourselves apart into a desert place, and rest a while:** for there were many coming and going, and they had no leisure so much as to eat. And they departed into a desert place by ship privately.* (Mark 6:31-32; King James Version—emphasis added)

Early in my Christian life and ministry I recall hearing Dr. Howard Hendricks say:

*You cannot be effective in ministry **to** people if you are always surrounded **by** people.*

The Bethsaida Personal Retreat follows a flurry of activity – rejection at Nazareth, sending out the twelve and the death of John the Baptist. The disciples couldn't burn the candle at both ends any better than we do – they needed to recharge. But they also needed a debriefing after returning from preaching and healing for the first time. They were understandably excited about the results of their ministry and simply needed a sharing time. Such times were essential to building their relationship with the Lord. The Bethsaida Personal Retreat provided that opportunity as well.

AFTER FEEDING THE 5000

Feeding the 5000 stands as one of the most familiar miracles of Christ. Note that the Bethsaida Personal Retreat immediately preceded this miracle. Is it just a coincidence that one of Christ's greatest miracles follows that time alone with the Father? I think not. But now another Personal Retreat *follows* the feeding of the 5000. John tells us the motivation of this retreat:

Perceiving then that they were about to come and take him by force to make him king, Jesus withdrew again to the mountain by himself. (John 6:15)

He had to get away from the crowd. Though I've never had to do a Personal Retreat because a mob wanted to make me king, I have many times had to get away from the crowd.

Those times alone keep one's perspective. Mark emphasizes Jesus sending the disciples across the Sea of Galilee:

Immediately he made his disciples get into the boat and go before him to the other side, to Bethsaida, while he dismissed the crowd. And after he had taken leave of them, he went up on the mountain to pray. (Mark 6:45-46)

Now the question arises as how Jesus could send them to Bethsaida when they were already there. Scholars generally think there were two Bethsaidas. Bethsaida Julias was on the northeast shore of the Sea of Galilee. This is probably where the Bethsaida Personal Retreat and the feeding of the 5000 took place. Bethsaida of Galilee was probably very close to Capernaum on the north shore. Some commentators feel the whole area may have been called Bethsaida in addition to the town of Bethsaida Julias.

Is it any surprise that yet another miracle follows this Personal Retreat? From the mountain above the lake, Jesus sees the disciples straining against the oars in a contrary wind. Assuming he was not using supernatural ability to see them, it was evening and not totally dark yet. But Jesus continues his time of communion with the Father for many hours, not coming to rescue the disciples until the fourth watch between three and six in the morning. Though he watches over us and sees our need, God still allows us to struggle before he rescues us.

When Jesus comes to the rescue, he comes supernaturally by walking on the water. Why did he choose to walk on the water? Was this just the easy way to get across the lake? Was he so full of the Father after his time on the mountain that walking on the water was almost automatic? Was this yet another teaching to the disciples of his divinity? Or was it just to show them his care wherever they were? Matthew Henry comments:

> . . . *Christ's approach to them in this condition; and in this we have an instance of his goodness, that he went unto them, as one that took cognizance of their case, and was under a concern about the church and people of God is Christ's opportunity to visit them and appear for them.*[5]

Again we see the pattern affirmed: Personal Retreats often precede events of major significance.

THE TRANSFIGURATION

The Transfiguration of Christ ranks as a miracle of miracles, unique in the Gospels. The story is reported in all three synoptic Gospels. We know the story, but do we really comprehend its significance? This is not just a spectacle, a divine light show, provided for the spiritual entertainment of the three disciples. The Transfiguration follows the Personal Retreat template:

> *Now about eight days after these sayings he took with him Peter and John and James and went up on the mountain to pray.* (Luke 9:28)

While Matthew and Mark say Jesus took them up the mountain to be by themselves, only Luke adds the purpose of prayer. The Son of God leads the disciples to a time away, they go to a remote place and something very important is about to happen.

What's the purpose of the Transfiguration? I always thought it was just for a testimony to Peter, James and John as they saw Christ glorified and heard the Father's voice affirming the Son's divinity. Certainly seeing Moses and Elijah talking to him affirmed that he was the fulfillment of Messianic prophecy. As an aside I would note that only Luke records the fact that the disciples were asleep previous to the event – a persistent problem that is recorded later at Gethsemane. There is some humor in between the lines here, as this was one prayer meeting they could not sleep through:

> *Now Peter and those who were with him were heavy with sleep, but when they became **fully awake** [emphasis added] they saw his glory and the two men who stood with him.* (Luke 9:32)

As I have reflected on this passage, I now think this miraculous event was not primarily for the disciples benefit. They were just onlookers – eavesdroppers. The main beneficiary was Jesus himself. Only in Luke do we read of the conversation between Jesus, Moses and Elijah:

> *And behold, two men were talking with him, Moses and Elijah, who appeared in glory and spoke of his departure, which he was about to accomplish at Jerusalem.* (Luke 9:10)

The glorified Moses and Elijah were sent to discuss with the incarnate God the Son the redemption of the world. What I wouldn't give to have been present for that discussion! I see this primarily as an **exhortation** to Jesus. Just as angels were dispatched by the Father to minister to Christ after his temptation, so Moses and Elijah, representing the Law and the Prophets, were sent to affirm Jesus' mission. The classic nineteenth century Jamieson, Fausset & Brown commentary beautifully captures this moment:

What now may be gathered from this statement? **(1)**
That a dying Messiah is the great article of the true
Jewish theology. *For a long time the Church* [i. e.
the Jewish nation before Christ's advent] *had fallen*
clean away from the faith of this article, and even from
a preparedness to receive it. But here we have that
jewel raked out of the dunghill of Jewish traditions,
and by the true representatives of the Church of old
made the one subject of talk with Christ Himself.
(2) The adoring gratitude of glorified men for His
undertaking to accomplish such a decease; their
felt dependence upon it for the glory in which they
appeared; their profound interest in the progress of
it, their humble solaces and encouragements to go
through with it; and their sense of its peerless and
overwhelming glory. *"Go, matchless, adored One, a*
Lamb to the slaughter! Rejected of men, but chosen
of God and precious; dishonored, abhorred, and
soon to be slain by men, but worshipped by cherubim,
ready to be greeted by all heaven. In virtue of that
decease we are here; our all is suspended on it and
wrapped up in it. Thine every step is watched by us
with ineffable interest; and though it were too high an
honor to us to be permitted to drop a word of cheer
into that precious but now clouded spirit, yet, as the
first fruits of harvest; the very joy set before him, we
cannot choose but tell Him that what is the depth of
shame to Him is covered with glory in the eyes of
heaven, that the Cross to Him is the Crown to us, that
that 'decease' is all our salvation and all our desire."
And who can doubt that such a scene **did** *minister*

deep cheer to that spirit? 'Tis said they "talked" not to Him, but "with Him"; and if they told Him how glorious His decease was, might He not fitly reply, "I know it, but your voice, as messengers from heaven come down to tell it Me, is music in Mine ears." [6] [emphases added]

Does it seem strange that mere men like Moses and Elijah should provide encouragement to God himself, the second person of the Trinity? This is again the mystery of the *kenosis*. Though fully God, Jesus temporarily laid aside his divine attributes for the limitations of flesh and blood. He is truly the second Adam in that human body, fully capable of emotion, pain, temptation, and even failure, just as the first Adam. The Epistle to the Hebrews makes this point perfectly clear:

For we do not have a high priest who is unable to sympathize with our weaknesses, but one who in every respect has been tempted as we are, yet without sin. (Heb. 4:15)

To say that Jesus was tempted but didn't sin is to admit that he could have sinned. Otherwise the above passage makes no sense. He could have failed, but thank God he didn't. Again, it's very easy in our zeal for orthodoxy to maintain the teaching of Jesus' divinity while downplaying his display of perfect humanity. But though he was both fully God and fully man, his humanity shows us the way to live as God intended.

The Transfiguration thus shows a major purpose for Personal Retreats: **encouragement from God**. Many times I've gone to a retreat doubting almost everything about my life and calling only to return encouraged by my encounter with God. If Jesus needed this intimate and dramatic assurance before going to the cross, do we need it any less?

GETHSEMANE

Christ spent his final Personal Retreat in the Garden of Gethsemane. Though it involved a relatively brief time, it was perhaps the most significant retreat in its impact. Scripture shares an unusual amount of detail as to his state of mind and his actual prayer to his Father, as given in the synoptic Gospels. The Gospel of John, having spent an entire chapter on his preceding high priestly prayer, only mentions Jesus going into the garden (John 18:1), but gives no details. Gethsemane is a Personal Retreat for deliverance:

> *And he withdrew from them about a stone's throw, and knelt down and prayed, saying, "Father, if you are willing, remove this cup from me. Nevertheless, not my will, but yours, be done." And there appeared to him an angel from heaven, strengthening him. And being in an agony he prayed more earnestly; and his sweat became like great drops of blood falling down to the ground.* (Luke 22:41-44)

The human incarnate God the Son does not want to go to the cross. If this prayer doesn't show Christ's perfect humanity, nothing does. He felt pain and tempted by fear, yet he obediently submits his request for deliverance to the Father's will.

Jesus shows us what to do when confronted with a formidable situation – spend intense time with God in prayer. Pour out your heart honestly as he did, confessing your fears and doubts. But ultimately yield the matter to the will of the sovereign God. It's okay to desire deliverance from life's excruciating trials as long as we remember that God's purposes are frequently fulfilled by *not* answering our pleas.

Let me again point out that Jesus in his incarnation has laid aside his divine attributes taking the role of a bondservant. He does not have omniscience at this point and does not know that his death on the cross is the *only* way. Otherwise, he would not pray as he does, "**If** you are willing, remove this cup." At this point he only knows what the Father has revealed to him. We are no different. But will we sweat great drops of blood in prayer to seek God, to seek understanding, to seek his will?

What were the results of this Personal Retreat? In response to Jesus' prayer, an angel came and ministered to him (Luke 22:43) in his agony, but he suffered and died according to the Father's will he submitted to. He did not shrink from the Father's eternal plan. He completed the course, crying from the cross, "It is finished" (John 19:30).

Even in the agony of Gethsemane, Jesus sought to teach Peter, James and John to pray as he did, but they slept. They missed the opportunity for the world's greatest teacher to show them how to commune with God in a crisis. He also sought the encouragement and power of their prayers to help carry him through his most difficult hours. They failed to be there for him. They had cut a very important class. Do we not do the same? When we fail to spend focused time alone with God at the critical moments of our lives, we cheat ourselves out of great blessings.

CONCLUSION

Though the Scriptures teach much about Personal Retreats with many biblical characters, we really need to go no farther than Jesus Christ to learn this concept. As in all areas of life and faith, he is our supreme example. We see in Christ the whole concept demonstrated and powerfully applied. The only reason we are here as Christians in the twenty-first century after his earthly ministry stems from his many Personal Retreats. Imagine where we would be if the wrong twelve apostles had been chosen, if he had not met with Moses and Elijah on the Mount of Transfiguration, if he had not regularly communed on isolated mountaintops with the Father and if he had not been strengthened to fulfill his destiny on the cross.

God the Son needed and craved those special times with his Father in heaven. If the incarnate God required those Personal Retreats to maintain his spiritual life, could we fail to see their necessity?

One simple exercise allows us to more fully capture the power of a Personal Retreat. Without it, Personal Retreats don't really work. Time to talk about journaling.

FOR FURTHER THOUGHT & DISCUSSION

1. What does the truth of Christ's perfect humanity teach you about Personal Retreats?

2. Why do you think that Jesus Christ so regularly needed Personal Retreats?

3. What applications do you draw from Christ's temptation in the wilderness?

4. How might a Personal Retreat help you make a major decision?

5. During a time of mourning, have you felt the need to get away by yourself? Why?

6. How might continual ministry activity without an occasional "face to face" with God, be counterproductive?

7. What was the benefit of Jesus getting away from the crowd after feeding the 5000?

8. What does viewing the Transfiguration as an exhortation to Christ tell you about God's purpose for Personal Retreats?

9. If Jesus, as God incarnate in a sinless human body, needs Personal Retreats, do you think you might also?

Chapter Six

Journaling: Transformation Captured

How many times have you been told to begin a journal? If you're anything like me, you've received that message multiple times. Journaling has uniquely deepened and transformed my life. It is an integral part of the Personal Retreat process that you dare not omit.

I started journaling as a daily spiritual discipline January 24, 2002. Of course I know that because that's the date on the first page of my first journal book! Though I had heard for years of the value of journaling, it took a Personal Coach to get me off the dime. My then pastor suggested Doug Peterson contact me for ideas on his new venture as a business consultant and personal coach. The original intent was that I would help Doug, but it turned out in reality he would help me far more.

The one word that would best describe my life at that point was **overwhelmed**. I was de-energized by my own disorganization. This was more than odd, given that most people think of me as an extremely ordered and organized person. I was in a rat race, and not being a rat, was most uncomfortable with that situation.

Doug laid out a plan for helping to better organize me and focus me on my goals. But the most significant thing he did was direct me to start a daily journal. He gave me a black journal book to start with, a book I'm looking at right now on my desk that started it all. I had but one assignment: Journal two minutes per day on my insights. Looking at that first journal today I am amazed at what God has done. My first entry reads:

*1/25/02 – The "Get it Done" system is working, giving me hope of being on top of my responsibilities. I was so encouraged by making progress with my desk, I cleaned out my desk trays that I have just been dumping things into for years. There were items there that were **six** years old! Never again! I'm getting free, and I'm going to stay that way.*

The journaling process developed quickly with more emphasis on Scripture and deeper insights into my own spiritual needs. On July 3, 2002 I wrote:

What will my epitaph say? I must ponder this question in detail, for answering it will transform my life. This much I know – If I were to lie dying today, I would feel a failure in many respects. Not because of lack of accomplishments, not because of lack of earnings or possessions, not because of lack of reputation – but because of lack of quality, intimate relationships. I feel a failure because of the superficiality of my communication and my usual inability to really "connect" with people.

I cannot begin to convey the warmth of blessing I experience today reading that entry, as so much in my life has changed in the intervening years. Presently I have twelve journal books covering eight years of my life. They are perhaps my most treasured possessions, recording God's working in perhaps the most difficult, yet blessed time of my life. But without those journals I would have scant memory of the great things the Lord has done.

Journaling particularly applies to Personal Retreats. I honestly doubt you can have a good retreat without journaling, for reasons I will outline in this chapter. Personal Retreats last at most a few days, but your journal can preserve that time with God for the rest of your life. What you get out of your Personal Retreats will largely depend on your journaling of those retreats.

WHAT IS JOURNALING?

How about the dictionary definition of a "journal":

A personal record of occurrences, experiences, and reflections kept on a regular basis; a diary.[1]

I see a journal a bit differently. For our purposes a journal is:

A recording of one's ongoing relationship with God for the purpose of enhancing spiritual growth.

91

A journal is not a diary. It is not an adolescent, narcissistic attempt at vanity over my own wonderfulness. Nor is it a mere recording of events and impressions, though it does entail that aspect. Likewise, a journal is not written for others to read. Nineteenth century French artist, Eugene Delacroix, said:

I am carrying out my plan, so long formulated, of keeping a journal. What I most keenly wish is not to forget that I am writing for myself alone. Thus I shall always tell the truth, I hope, and thus shall improve myself. These pages will reproach me for my changes of mind.[2]

When you begin to journal, abandon any vain thought that you're a celebrity and someone's going to make a movie from your journal! You probably weren't thinking that anyway, but just in case I wanted to mention it.

Having stressed the privacy of your journal, there are exceptions in which it should be shared. It may be appropriate to share an impression from the Lord with a friend, a Bible study or anyone needing that particular exhortation. I would also want my journals to be for the edification of my wife (if I predecease her) and especially as a spiritual heritage for my children. Many great believers of the past continue to bless the Church today because we can read their journals. For example the Autobiography of George Muller is essentially a journal of God's answers to prayer on behalf of the orphans he served. You can likewise leave a spiritual legacy through your journals, particularly for your own descendants. Nevertheless, your primary focus in keeping a journal should be that it would serve you during your life.

Having described what a journal is not, what is a journal? A journal is a recording of what you are saying to God, both by way of praise and petition. But, moreover, it's a recording of what God is saying to you. A journal records your struggles and crying out to God. It records your prayers of petition as well as your prayers of thanksgiving. I find much of my journal features Bible verses through which God has spoken to me on that particular day. But a journal also records God's voice from other sources – devotionals, other Christian books, exhortations from friends, from sermons – you name it.

Ultimately a journal is simply a testimonial of God's work in your life. Maurice Blanchot wrote:

The Journal is not essentially a confession, a story about oneself. It is a Memorial. What does the writer have to remember? Himself, who he is when he is not writing, when he is living his daily life, when he is alive and real, and not dying and without truth.[3]

What is he saying? He emphasizes that journaling is about internalizing that often elusive commodity – truth. I particularly like what Scottish author, James Boswell said:

As a lady adjusts her dress before a mirror, a man adjusts his character by looking at his journal.[4]

Do you dare to see who you really are? Start journaling.

DAVID'S JOURNAL

Not until writing this chapter did I realize that the Psalms are David's Journal. Though David wasn't the sole author of the Psalms, he wrote the majority of them. It's no small wonder then that I find myself frequently quoting the Psalms in my own journal. The Psalms provide a wonderful model for what a truly good and effective journal should look like. The more your journal entries are looking like the Psalms the better.

The Psalms typically begin with David speaking to God by way of complaint and petition. As he expresses his thoughts, God begins to speak to him, usually resulting with praise as the psalm concludes. David's "journal" is the raw, unvarnished truth of his heart, void of pretense. He tells it like it is, yet is ever so receptive to the correcting and exhorting voice of God in his spirit.

Let's look at this pattern. David writes Psalm 3 as he is fleeing from his own son, Absalom, who is trying to usurp the throne:

O Lord, how many are my foes! Many are rising against me; many are saying of my soul, there is no salvation for him in God. But you, O lord, are a shield about me, my glory, and the lifter of my head. I cried aloud to the Lord, and he answered me from his holy hill. (Ps. 3:1-4)

You may not appreciate that Psalm unless you've really have people out to destroy you as he did. As an alternative medicine practitioner using cutting edge approaches, I have seldom had a time when some government bureaucrat or envious competitor wasn't trying to destroy me in their own stupidity and arrogance. It was the same in my vocational Christian ministry on college campuses as a young adult. Taking a stand for God's truth, as David repeatedly did, provides a life blessed with affliction . . . and blessed with the intimate presence of God.

Psalm 51 was David's journal entry in a very different situation. Nathan, the Prophet, had just confronted him with his sin of adultery with Bathsheba and the murder of her husband, Uriah:

Have mercy on me, Oh God, according to your

steadfast love; according to your abundant mercy blot out my transgressions. Wash me thoroughly from my iniquity, and cleanse me from my sin! Let me hear joy and gladness; let the bones that you have broken rejoice. Hide your face from my sins, and blot out all my iniquities. Create in me a clean heart, O God, and renew a right spirit within me. Cast me not away from your presence, and take not your Holy Spirit from me. Restore to me the joy of your salvation, and uphold me with a willing spirit. (Ps. 51:1-2, 8-12)

Sometimes a journal embodies confession of sin and the restoration and forgiveness of God. A good journal records the highs as well as the lows.

In the wilderness of Judah David wrote Psalm 63. It sounds like this time away fits our definition of a Personal Retreat:

O God, you are my God; earnestly I seek you; my soul thirsts for you in a dry and weary land where there is no water. (Ps. 63:1)

Can't you just imagine David wandering out into the Judean wilderness talking to God and deepening his relationship with the Lord? David is always seeking God from the depths of his being. Is it any wonder he was called a man after God's own heart?

The "journal entry" of Psalm 142 finds David hiding in a cave, either Adullam (1 Sam. 22:1) or Engedi (1 Sam. 24:1-3). As was so common in his life, he is fleeing his enemies, yet all the while trusting God:

With my voice I cry out to the Lord; with my voice I plead for mercy to the Lord. I pour out my complaint

before him; I tell my trouble before him . . . Attend to
my cry, for I am brought very low! Deliver me from
my persecutors, for they are too strong for me!
(Ps. 142:1-2, 6)

Do you pick up the genuineness of this relationship David has with God? He lets it all hang out – the complaints, the prayers, the praise, the rejoicing. David was gut level honest with God. Because he wrote the journal of the Psalms, we can see today what a deep relationship with God looks like.

BENEFITS OF JOURNALING

We do things for the benefits we receive – desire for gain, as well as fear of loss. If you believe the benefits of journaling, you will start journaling. Once you experience those benefits, you will never stop journaling. I know this to be true, because of my own experience. I haven't stopped journaling in eight years. What this simple activity does for me is so amazing that I can't wait to write another entry.

Now compare that with the way most Christians see spiritual activities: "Well, I don't really enjoy _____ [you fill in the blank], but I'm supposed to do this, so I guess I will . . . maybe." Fill in that blank with reading the Bible, having a Quiet Time, giving, witnessing or whatever. If you're not intrinsically motivated to do something, if there isn't a burning desire driving you to that activity, you're wasting your time. Bottom line, we do what we see benefit in doing.

That benefit is not always an immediate Damascus Road experience, however. You may need to commit yourself by faith to journaling for a couple of weeks before you truly experience the desired benefits. My conviction is that anyone who is seriously committed to knowing God intimately will be thrilled with the experience of journaling in fairly short order. But you have to begin – you have to try it.

So what are some specific benefits of journaling? Let's look at five of them.

BENEFIT #1 –REMEMBERING

How often have you had a great idea and then forgotten it before you could write it down? That happens to me all the time. With me it's usually a book idea, a title, or some scriptural insight. Whatever it is, if I don't capture it on paper fast, it's gone. Sometimes it comes back, but often I never have that insight again. At any age we forget, but the older we are, more problematic this is:

> *To have some account of my thoughts, manners, acquaintance and actions, when the hour arrives in which time is more nimble than memory, is the reason which induces me to keep a journal: a journal in which I must confess my every thought, must open my whole heart!*[5]

A journal preserves the insights God gives you. I am so blessed by periodically going back and reading what issues were on my heart years ago, and how God spoke to me then. To reread those entries now is like reading something altogether new, even though I wrote it. The Holy Spirit can (and often does) anoint your words of years gone by to give them fresh meaning.

Think about it: What if Moses and the other prophets never wrote down what we now call the Bible? Would we have retained that memory through the millennia? Would we have the sure word from God we have today? I doubt it. Our entire faith rests on the fact that men inspired by the Holy Spirit wrote down their encounters with the living God (2 Pet. 1:19-21). Make no mistake—neither your journal nor mine will ever be Scripture. God has finished the Bible. But that doesn't mean he doesn't still speak to his children in the quiet of the heart as reflected on the pages of their journals.

BENEFIT #2 –ANCHORING

Truth is fleeting, so how do we hang on to it? How do we anchor the truth firmly to our souls? To understand this, we have to review "learning styles." Different people learn and retain things differently. Some are **auditory**. They learn wonderfully from a classroom lecture or a sermon. Parenthetically, let me say these were the kids that always excelled in school. They were the "A" students that passed all the tests with flying colors, the ones the teachers loved. Classroom education is predicated on the false assumption that everyone learns by hearing.

Others are **visual** learners. They learn by seeing and by reading. These people may not get much out of the lecture, but if they can see it written down in the book, the brain starts working. Since most classroom education has a visual element, these folks generally do okay in school.

The problems usually manifest the most with the third learning style – **kinesthetic** – learning by doing. Kinesthetic people don't learn by hearing or seeing something, but by getting their hands on it. Their memory is stored in their muscles. Because of this, kinesthetic learners love movement. Enter the typical Attention Deficit Hyperactive Disorder (ADHD) child. These kids are the round pegs in the square holes of the school system. They're labeled "troublemakers" and drugged into submission. But actually they're just operating in a different paradigm than the "one size fits all" of the typical school.

So what do learning styles have to do with journaling? Simply this: Employing all three learning styles will drive God's truths into your heart more deeply. You can hear a Scripture or spiritual truth or see it in a Bible or a book. But you really anchor that truth when you get that third learning style of body movement involved by writing it down. That cements it somehow. Writing insights down in a journal integrates the idea into your heart much more readily than just hearing or seeing it in writing. Employing all three learning styles results in a manifold increase in retention.

Almost daily I record scripture verses and quotes from various devotional books in my journal. I record what God impresses me with, and by that I am capturing those particular truths. I am driving them down to a deeper level—anchoring them. Just reading can go in one ear and out the other, or maybe I should say in one eye and out the other. But once you start slowly writing it down something happens. I am making that truth a prisoner of my heart.

The act of writing passages down in and of itself deepens understanding. I get insights while I'm writing as I more fully grasp the meaning, a meaning I missed in quickly scanning over those same words. The required slowing involved in writing a verse down fosters illumination.

May I also emphasize the application of this same principle to prayer? Verbal and visual prayers are often fleeting, but writing it down intensifies the meaning of the words. It's the difference between a taste and downing the whole glass. We live in world of constant, high-speed inputs – the "noise" we talked about in a previous chapter. The simple act of writing in a journal slows down and focuses the inputs. It allows you to begin hearing God's voice over the din of a neurotically noisy world.

BENEFIT #3 – REPEATING

All of us learn and have learned by repetition. Journals allow repetition as you have the opportunity to reread an entry multiple times. Let's face it, no matter what the venue, we seldom get the whole message the first time. The more we repeat a message, the more we water it that it might take root.

How often did your parents repeat instruction to you like, "Don't play in the street," "Look both ways before you cross," and the like? As parents raising children we assume lots of repetition is required. This is also a principle in sales. Any good salesman knows you keep repeating your key points. Customers don't get it the first time. A salesman knows that probably 90 percent of what you hear you will forget unless you repeat it—especially if you repeat it by writing it down.

Look at how many things Christ repeated to the disciples, especially during those final hours:

If you love me, you will keep my commandments. (John 14:15)

Whoever has my commandments and keeps them, he it is who loves me. (John 14:21a)

If anyone loves me, he will keep my word . . . (John 14:23a)

Whoever does not love me does not keep my words.
(John 14:24a)

If the personification of truth, the Son of God, taught by repetition, can we do less in teaching ourselves?

BENEFIT #4 – ENCOURAGING

When you're on a trip, do you ever look at a map to see where you've come from and where you're going? A journal similarly records your spiritual journey. Where have I come from spiritually? What progress have I made? What victories have been won? How have I matured? How has God shown his faithfulness? Your journal answers all these questions. I never reread one of my old journals from past years without being encouraged. It's not that the struggles recorded have since gone away. In fact, sometimes they've gotten worse! It's not that I see myself as so much more mature now than I was when I wrote those words. Sometimes I spiritually regress. It's simply that I see God continuing his work in me, whether in my journal of five years ago or today, encouraging me with his faithfulness.

BENEFIT #5 – UNLOADING

Journaling helps unload our burdens. Just as talking to a friend provides relief, so does journaling. In it you are sharing those burdens with yourself and God – hopefully your two best friends! You will be amazed at how much journaling relieves the excruciating pressures of life.

The Psalms again set the example, in showing a progression from burden to relief. David's problems didn't go away because he journaled a Psalm, but writing it down made a difference – a difference in perspective and resulting peace. Take Psalm 13 as an example:

How long, O Lord? Will you forget me forever? How long will you hide your face from me? How long must I take counsel in my soul and have sorrow in my heart all the day? How long shall my enemy be exalted over me? Consider and answer me, O Lord my God; light up my eyes, lest I sleep the sleep of death, lest my enemy say, "I have prevailed over him," lest my foes rejoice because I am shaken. But I have trusted in your steadfast love; my heart shall rejoice in your salvation. I will sing to the Lord, because he has dealt bountifully with me.

David started this "journal entry" sobbing; he ended it singing. That is my experience as well. Baring my heart to the Lord in my journal made way for the reassurance of his presence.

JOURNALING A PERSONAL RETREAT

So far I've only spoken of journaling in general – the kind of journaling I do daily in my quiet time. Journaling on a Personal Retreat is a little different, though it will come naturally if you've been doing it in your daily routine. Let me emphasize up front that, in my opinion, journaling makes or breaks your "face to face" encounter on a Personal Retreat. Journaling decides whether your retreat will be **recreation** or **transformation.** Without journaling I predict your insights will be superficial at best. Remember, a Personal Retreat is fundamentally an **encounter with God.** Journaling allows you to capture that encounter and deepen every insight.

A familiar passage in James teaches this principle:

But be doers of the word, and not hearers only, deceiving yourselves. For if anyone is a hearer of the word and not a doer, he is like a man who looks intently at his natural face in a mirror. For he looks at himself and goes away and at once forgets what he was like. But the one who looks into the perfect law of liberty, and perseveres, being no hearer who forgets but a doer who acts, he will be blessed in his doing. (James 1:22-25)

So what's the point? Only hearing is quickly forgotten, while doing transforms. The various inputs received on a Personal Retreat are "hearing," but journaling is definitely in the "doing" category – it's work! But it's work you will love the fruit of.

THE CENTRAL ACTIVITY

Journaling is the central activity of a Personal Retreat around which everything else revolves. My journal becomes the guide leading me through my retreat. I start with my journal asking the question, "Why am I here?" What needs have driven me to this time away and alone with God? Those initial entries at the beginning of a Personal Retreat set the stage for all that follows as your mind and spirit process the questions. Insights to record in your journal will come through thoughts, Scripture you read, books you read and prayers you pray. After a period of clearing the "noise," you will be amazed at all of the things you want to write down. Make entries in your journal as if doing that is the only way you're going to permanently possess that insight—because it probably is! And when it starts flowing, let it flow and just keep writing.

Journaling intensifies the impact of your Personal Retreat. As we've already discussed, just writing things down will make you think more deeply. This is only logical, in that you've slowed the input process. We think at many thousands of words per minute. Most of us read only hundreds of words per minute at best. But you write only a handful of words per minute. Does that allow for a more thorough and deeper thought process? Absolutely!

WRITING OR KEYBOARD?

Let's address a very practical question: Does a journal have to be handwritten or can it be typed into your computer? I don't have a hard and fast answer. I have always written my journals long hand. I think the slower speed of writing is helpful for better absorbing and meditating on the entries. Though I would never hand write for a book or an article, there's something about my journal that I prefer writing by hand. Maybe a computer file is just too impersonal for the deeply personal experience of journaling, particularly journaling a Personal Retreat.

On the paranoia side of the question, I know I won't likely lose the hand written journal – I wish I could say the same for every file I've saved on my computer! I also never have to worry about losing battery power. Overall, this may be largely a question of personality, of "different strokes for different folks." If you want to try journaling electronically, go ahead and see how it works. Compare it with handwriting and see which works best for you.

PRESERVING THE IMPACT

A journal is a record of your relationship with God – you speaking to him and him speaking to you. Without a journal it's difficult to impossible to relive and reclaim the insights of a previous Personal Retreat. Just thinking back I couldn't tell you offhand what I learned on Personal Retreats I took five years ago or even two months ago. But I can flip over to those pages in my journal and discover again the voice of God in my life. A journal lets you have the benefit of a Personal Retreat again and again. But it also drops a plumb line to test your maturity. When you look back at your journal of a previous retreat, do you see growth? Have you progressed beyond the issues that troubled you then? Have you seen God's answers and intervention in those previous concerns of your heart?

All this presumes you actually reread your journals – a practice I often find myself negligent in. One of the best ways to preserve the impact is to begin a Personal Retreat rereading one or more of your previous journals. You will be amazed at how much you've forgotten, as well as blessed by the insights that have continued in your life. We need to be reminded of what we already know. That was Peter's message to the first century church:

> *Therefore I intend always to **remind** you of these qualities, though you know them and are established in the truth that you have. I think it right, as long as I am in this body, to stir you up by way of **reminder**, since I know that the putting off of my body will be soon, as our Lord Jesus Christ made clear to me. And I will make every effort so that after my departure you may be able at any time to **recall** these things.*
> (2 Pet. 1:12-15)

Once you experience the profound effect of a Personal Retreat, you will do everything possible to preserve its impact. Journaling best accomplishes that goal.

SIMPLE STEPS TO JOURNALING

I hope I've conveyed the profound importance of journaling. But how do you begin? Here are some steps:

1. Buy a Journal Book – You get these at office supply stores (unless you're doing your journal on your computer). A journal book has lined pages and nothing else. You'll put in your own dates.

2. Add Journaling to Your Quiet Time – Journaling is not just for Personal Retreats. Its true impact comes from daily use. Of course, if you're not having a daily devotional time, it's high time you started. If you're going to have any kind of a maturing, deepening relationship with God, you have to spend time daily in the Bible, in prayer and perhaps also in a devotional book.

There are many ways of doing a quiet time. I read one Psalm per day or one chapter of Proverbs to begin with. Then I read the day's selection from books like Oswald Chamber's *My Utmost for His Highest* or Charles Spurgeon's *Morning and Evening*. I've also been greatly blessed by a devotional oriented toward business people, *Today God is First* by Os Hillman. There are many devotional resources available. Find one or two you like and use them.

Write in your journal what impresses you from the various sources you're reading. Write down your concerns, worries and frustrations, as well as your petitions to God. Make your journal a conversation with a friend – which indeed it is. Honestly pour out your heart and gratefully receive the peace, presence and illumination of the Holy Spirit.

Daily journaling makes for an easy transition to journaling a Personal Retreat. As a matter of fact our word "journal" comes from the Latin word for "daily." To be really effective a journal must become part of your daily routine. Once you've established the habit of journaling, I'm betting you'll be hooked for life.

3. Journaling on a Personal Retreat – There's not a lot of difference between journaling on a Personal Retreat as compared to your daily journal. Again, I would begin by writing down your concerns. What has driven you to this Personal Retreat? I like to number those questions or issues – #1, #2, #3, etc. After laying out my heartfelt needs in the journal, I wait for God to meet me – I wait for the encounter with God. I may begin with taking a nap if I'm tired from the effort of getting to my retreat location. I may start reading the Bible or a Christian book I've brought along. I may go out and take a leisurely walk – a "stop and smell the roses" type of walk. I divorce myself from time and hurry and busyness and simply practice being the Lord's child, relaxing and delighting in his presence.

Start writing again in your journal when insights start coming. Maybe there's a Scripture passage that really strikes you with its relevancy to your situation. Or maybe it's something from the book you're reading. Or maybe it's an insight gained by the increasing awareness of the world around you – a bird in flight, a squirrel scurrying across the campsite, the intricacies of a spider web touched with the morning dew. As you "tune in" to this sanctified spot where God is meeting with you, the noise in your head will dissipate and insights will flow. And your journal will capture the transformation – a transformation dependent on our next subject – prayer.

FOR FURTHER THOUGHT & DISCUSSION

1. If you've thought about keeping a journal, what has stopped you?

2. How might journaling help your spiritual life?

3. Have you had special insights only to forget them for lack of writing them down?

4. Do you believe your thoughts and impressions from God are worth writing down? Why or why not?

5. What benefits would you expect to receive from daily journaling?

6. Would you commit to journaling a few minutes every day for one month?

Chapter Seven

A Different Way to Pray

Just as we learn journaling to intensify our relationship with God, so we must learn prayer, or more typically, *relearn* prayer. Prayer is the life-blood of your meeting with God—it is fundamentally what a Personal Retreat is all about. The whole point is to talk with God, to encounter him. An inability to effectively pray cripples your time away. Unfortunately you will never truly encounter God with the kind of prayer most Christians pray. The good news, though, is that Personal Retreats will teach you this different way to pray.

So, this is the question: Do we really know how to pray? Are you satisfied with your prayer life? I know no Christian who is. I feel no greater deficiency after nearly forty years knowing Christ than in my ability to pray. It unquestionably ranks as the weakest area of my Christian life. To say I feel disqualified to write this chapter is an understatement.

Yet through Personal Retreats I have *begun* to discover a deeper, more quality conversation with God – a different way to pray. I emphasize the word *begun*, for this is a work very much still in progress in my life. But I have great hope of seeing the promised completion of the Spirit's work in me in this area as well (Phil. 1:6).

"TEACH US TO PRAY"

I find it fascinating that the disciples had only one teaching request from the Lord. They did *not* ask, "Teach us to preach," or "Teach us to study the Scriptures," or "Teach us to be wise." And they definitely did *not* ask, "Teach us to love and serve." Their lone teaching request was, "Teach us to pray."

> *Now Jesus was praying in a certain place, and when he finished, one of his disciples said to him, "Lord, teach us to pray, as John taught his disciples."*
> (Luke 11:1)

What was it about Jesus' prayer life that was so enticing? What did they hear in his conversations with the Father that they wanted? Why did hearing Jesus pray make such an impression? I believe it was the *relational* nature of his prayers. Scripture records two instances of Jesus' words in prayer. The first is the High Priestly Prayer of John 17:

> *When Jesus had spoken these words, he lifted up his eyes to heaven, and said, "Father, the hour has come; glorify your Son that the Son may glorify you, since you have given him authority over all flesh, to give eternal life to all whom you have given him. And this is eternal life, that they know you the only true God, and Jesus Christ whom you have sent. I glorified*

you on earth, having accomplished the work that you gave me to do. And now, Father, glorify me in your own presence with the glory that I had with you before the world existed. (John 17:1-5)

We look at this very familiar passage and so easily miss the point. Imagine the audacity of calling God his Father? The Pharisees took major issue with that often repeated practice of Jesus. Do we ever see anyone in the Old Testament calling God "Father?" Jesus introduced intimacy with God, and that intimacy is the most striking aspect of the High Priestly Prayer. He is speaking to someone he really knows. He shows us by his prayer life the God who is near.

Look at the progression of the prayer: Jesus' initial focus is on the glory of God. Then he prays for the protection of the disciples. The prayer ends with Jesus including the disciples in relationship with the Father and Son, a prayer request that includes us:

I do not ask for these only, but also for those who will believe in me through their word, that they may all be one, just as you, Father, are in me, and I in you, that they also may be in us, so that the world may know that you sent me and loved them even as you loved me. Father, I desire that they also, whom you have given me, may be with me where I am, to see my glory that you have given me because you loved me before the foundation of the world. (John 17:20-24)

Once we receive Christ as our Savior we say that we "know the Lord," but do we really know the Lord? You can know the Lord, but then you can also know the Lord. There are degrees of knowing, and the knowing we see in this passage is a most intimate sort of knowing. The disciples stood amazed at someone who could talk to God this way. Just as he taught them, so he will teach us to pray.

Soon after the High Priestly Prayer the Bible again lets us eavesdrop on the prayer life of Jesus in the Garden of Gethsemane:

> *And he withdrew from them about a stone's throw, and knelt down and prayed, saying, "Father, if you are willing, remove this cup from me. Nevertheless, not my will, but yours be done." And there appeared to him an angel from heaven, strengthening him. And being in an agony he prayed more earnestly; and his sweat became like great drops of blood falling down to the ground.* (Luke 22:41-44)

This is a prayer of spiritual battle as Jesus discerned what was about to happen. Likewise it is a prayer of desperation in which the thought of the coming separation from the Father apparently ruptured capillaries. As discussed in Chapter 3, the Son of God voluntarily subjected himself to the limitations of life in a human body. He tasted the agony of the wrath of God for our souls. Here we gaze upon a moment like none other in time or eternity. Yet in spite of the incomprehensible pain, Jesus ultimately prays surrendering to the Father's will.

How far I am from this kind of prayer, yet how very compelling it is. I am often desperate for God's presence in my life, but I have not yet sweat drops of blood. But what an encouragement to know that in life's battles I can pour out my soul to God in full surrender to his will, knowing that is enough.

To speak of Jesus and prayer probably first suggests what has come to be known in the church as "The Lord's Prayer." That title is a bit erroneous since this is a prayer

Jesus never prayed. It is more correctly referred to as "The Disciples' Prayer," though I think it is best described as "The Model Prayer." Jesus never told them to pray this prayer, but rather told them "Pray *like* this." Thus it is a model, an outline of what prayer should look like. This prayer comes in an interesting context: Jesus gave this model to rebuke vain prayers of unbelievers:

> *And when you pray, do not heap up empty phrases as the Gentiles do, for they think that they will be heard for their many words. Do not be like them, for your Father knows what you need before you ask him. Pray then like this:*
>
> > *Our Father in heaven, hallowed be your name. Your kingdom come, your will be done, on earth as it is in heaven. Give us this day our daily bread, and forgive us our debts, as we also have forgiven our debtors, and lead us not into temptation, but deliver us from evil.*

So what are the elements of the Model Prayer? Right off the bat we again see intimacy with God in addressing him as "Father." Praise follows for God's attribute of holiness, which in a way encompasses all of God's attributes. He is different from us; he is exalted and set apart whether we're talking about his holiness itself, or his transcendence, omnipotence, omniscience, grace, mercy, love, justice, etc. Next we pray for the coming of God's kingdom, for his rule to permeate the earth as it does heaven. Petition for daily provision is next. Note this is a prayer for survival needs, not luxurious wants. God promises to feed his kids, not to provide gourmet food in a 4000 square foot castle with a Lexus in the driveway. The model prayer concludes with confession of sin, prayer for forgiveness and petition for protection from temptation.

Somehow this prayer is rather different from the prayers Christians usually pray. It is intimate, but it is also basic and simple. It is focused on God – his glory, his kingdom, his will. It is a prayer that moves us toward an intimate relationship with God.

RELATIONAL PRAYER

You'll never deeply encounter God with the kind of prayer most Christians pray.

I recommend moving to what I call "Relational Prayer." Let me illustrate: You're a parent and you have a child. Imagine your child coming up to you and saying:

Dad (or Mom), I've decided I'm going to spend 15 minutes a day with you. I'm going to begin my day reading something you've written and also read some things others have written about you. Then I'm going to ask you for some things that I really believe you'll give me. I'm also going to occasionally thank you for some of the things you've already given me.

Suppose that is the entire relationship your child chooses to have with you. What would be your reaction as a parent? Wouldn't you be heartbroken? Why? You want a *relationship* not a ritual. You want actual contact and interaction. You want to do things together with your child. You want them to express their love toward you, not just use you.

Have you ever gone beyond the infantile state? What is the relationship a baby has with its parents? "Feed me. Change me. Hold me." "Feed me. Change me. Hold me." That's it. Now we expect that from a baby and delight in doing those things (maybe delight's not the word for the changing part, but you know what I mean). But when you should be mature, and all you want is God to meet your needs and to serve you; that's a problem.

Applying this to prayer, are we really any better than the idolaters of old praying to a block of wood? We must put the reality of *relationship* into our spiritual life – relationship not just ritual. What if you could relate to God like a child would to a loving parent? You can. We are his children, and he is our Father, though we act like he is anything but that. Discovering Relational Prayer will take us from a distant, ritualistic practice of our spirituality to a deep and intimate ongoing conversation with God.

We cry out for that father relationship that with so many people is lacking. No wonder we struggle with relating to God as Father with all its implications. John Eldredge shares some penetrating insights on our disconnection from God as our Father:

> *Our core assumptions about the world boil down to this: we are on our own to make life work. We are not watched over. We are not cared for . . . When we are hit with a problem, we have to figure it out ourselves, or just take the hit. If anything good is going to come our way, we're the ones who are going to have to arrange for it. Many of us have called upon God as Father, but, frankly, he doesn't seem to have heard. We're not sure why. Maybe we didn't do it right. Maybe he's about more important matters. Whatever the reason, our experience of this world has framed our approach to life. We believe we are fatherless.[1]*

Compare our "fatherlessness" with Jesus words:

> *Or which one of you, if his son asks him for bread, will give him a stone? Or if he asks for a fish, will give him a serpent? If you then, who are evil, know*

how to give good gifts to your children, how much more will your Father who is in heaven give good things to those who ask him! (Matt.7:9-11)

The Holy Spirit brings the message of the father relationship to our hearts:

And because you are sons, God has sent the Spirit of his Son into our hearts, crying, "Abba! Father! So you are no longer a slave, but a son, and if a son, then an heir through God." (Gal. 4:6-7)

To embrace Relational Prayer simply means conversing with God like he's your Father – because he is! Just enjoy being with him and doing things together. He is closer than you can imagine, so begin relating to him in that simple child-like faith.

PURPOSE OF PRAYER

At the heart of discovering this different way to pray is the question of prayer's purpose. What are we really doing when we pray? What exactly is prayer supposed to accomplish? Unfortunately most of our concepts of prayer are a little fuzzy at best. On the one hand we believe "prayer changes things," while on the other hand, if we know our Bible doctrine, we also know that God has ordained whatever comes to pass, as the Westminster Confession states:

God from all eternity did, by the most wise and holy counsel of his own will, freely and unchangeably ordain whatsoever comes to pass; yet so as thereby neither is God the author of sin, nor is violence offered to the will of the creatures, nor is the liberty or contingency of second causes taken away, but rather established.[2]

So what's really the point of prayer?

Prayer really doesn't change things, but rather does something far more important, as noted by Oswald Chambers:

> *It is not so true that "prayer changes things" as that prayer changes **me** and I change things. God has so constituted things that prayer on the basis of Redemption alters the way in which a man looks at things. Prayer is not a question of altering things externally, but of working wonders in a man's disposition.*[3]

Is prayer changing you, or are you still trying to change God with prayer?

The purpose of prayer is to come into communion with God—to come to know him intimately. Certain activities constitute "thin spots" where time and eternity intersect. Prayer is one of those "thin spots" where the life of God uniquely touches us. Oswald Chambers comments:

> *It is not part of the life of a natural man to pray. We hear it said that a man will suffer in his life if he does not pray; I question it. What will suffer is the life of the Son of God in Him, which is nourished not by food, but by prayer. When a man is born from above, the life of the Son of God is born in him, and he can either starve that life or nourish it. Prayer is the way the life of God is nourished. **Our ordinary views of prayer are not found in the New Testament. We look upon prayer as a means of getting things for ourselves; the Bible idea of prayer is that we may get to know God Himself.** [Emphasis added]*[4]

Chambers also comments:

> *The idea of prayer is not in order to get answers from God; prayer is perfect and complete oneness with God. If we pray because we want answers, we will get huffed with God. The answers come every time, but not always in the way we expect, and our spiritual huff shows a refusal to identify ourselves with our Lord in prayer. We are not here to prove God answers prayer; we are here to be living monuments of God's grace.[5]*

ALIGNMENT WITH GOD'S WILL

Prayer should align us with the will of God, rather than attempting to align God's will with our desires. A familiar verse discusses this:

> *And this is the confidence that we have toward him, that if we ask anything according to his will he hears us. And if we know that he hears us in whatever we ask, we know that we have the requests that we have asked of him.* (1 John 5:14-15)

I've lost track of the number of prayers I've heard "hedged" with "if it's your will." The point of John's exhortation is not to get us to tack that disclaimer on the end of every prayer, but to enter into the will of God *first*. How would your prayer life change if you *only* prayed for things that you *knew* were the will of God? Now that's a radical thought! Perhaps we should stick with praise and confession until we know God's will on a matter and only then graduate in our prayers to specific petitions. If you're in communion with God, you will know what his will is, for your will and his will then coincide. As someone in my

Sunday School class said, "If you have no will but his will, do whatever you will."

Perhaps we should focus more on praying for wisdom on the matters that burden us before presuming God needs to bail us out. After lauding the importance of trials in God's plan for our maturity, James declares a great promise:

If any of you lacks wisdom, let him ask of God, who gives generously to all without reproach, and it will be given him. (James 1:5)

Always remember that prayer primarily relates to what God is doing, not what I'm doing. Part of an old Puritan prayer goes like this:

Let me know that the work of prayer is to bring my will to thine, and that without this it is folly to pray; when I try to bring thy will to mine it is to command Christ, to be above him, and wiser than he: this is my sin and pride. I can only succeed when I pray according to thy precept and promise, and to be done with as it pleases thee, according to thy sovereign will.[6]

TALKING TO YOURSELF?

I've observed that many Christians pray like they're talking on the phone with their thumb on the receiver button. Rule #1 on telephone conversations is to **make connection before you start talking.** Otherwise, you're just talking to yourself. Personal Retreats have a way of establishing that connection. It's not that you can't establish that connection during a daily quiet time—it's just harder. Prayer, Bible reading and worship all may tune us into God and his will, but the "face to face" encounter of Personal Retreats, in an almost magical way, accentuates that process. Our usual prayer, Bible study and worship easily lose sight of the objective of encountering God, becoming ends in themselves. By contrast Personal Retreats begin with the understanding that I'm doing this to encounter God, to deeply commune with him.

So how do we go from our self-centered, petition-oriented prayers to prayers enhancing our relationship with our Father in heaven? Here are a few "rules" I've found helpful:

RULE #1 – LISTEN MORE

That's a polite way of saying, "You need to shut up more when you pray." There's far too much talking in our prayer and not enough listening. Andrew Murray wrote:

Take time. Give God time to reveal Himself to you. Give yourself time to be silent and quiet before Him, waiting to receive, through the Spirit, the assurance of His presence with you, His power working in you.[7]

I remember one particular client in my years of clinical practice that provided the most wonderful negative example of this. During her entire appointment she absolutely would not stop talking, going from one topic to another. I honestly don't know when she found time to breathe! Normally, as I am performing our computerized, non-invasive nutritional testing, I provide a running commentary of the tests and their results. Of course I talk because I know what's going on. I know the interpretation of the test results. My clients don't know that, so they usually mostly listen with an occasional clarifying question.

So what did I do? I just let her talk while I continued the testing. Though it was very annoying, I got the test results I needed. The problem is the client learned nothing, whereas she *could* have learned so much about the state of her health simply by listening more. She could have left my office with a much deeper understanding of her situation and what to do about it. Instead she left knowing no more than when she came in.

Get the parallel? Does our incessant jabbering in prayer nauseate God? Would he like to perhaps get a word in edgewise? Does he just let us keep talking and talking? Yes. Do we fail to hear his voice that we might learn and mature? Yes.

Beware of extremes. Note that I did not say, "Only listen," but "listen more," and there's a big difference. I am definitely *not* saying you should never speak to God, or that you should never ask him for things. Scripture is clear in commanding us to ask:

Ask, and it will be given to you; seek, and you will find; knock, and it will be opened to you. For everyone who asks receives, and the one who seeks finds, and to the one who knocks it will be opened. (Matt. 7:7-8)

You do not have because you do not ask. (James 4:2b)

We are to ask of God. The problem occurs when we ask incessantly without having first developed a relationship. Suppose you had never actually met your biological father, though you unquestionably are related. What if, out of the blue, you call him up and ask him to send you $1000. Wouldn't it be just like asking a stranger for $1000? But compare that with making the same request of an earthly father you've known and built a relationship with your entire life? You would probably get a very different response.

It's about relationship. Relational Prayer focuses on communion with God via listening more and talking less. As discussed in Chapter 5, we have to clear the noise in our heads. God is speaking, but we typically can't hear him over the noise of our own voice. Would that we approach the throne of God with great humility and contrition, ever aware of our comparative insignificance. I'm reminded of Solomon's words:

> *Guard your steps when you go to the house of God. To draw near to listen is better than to offer the sacrifice of fools, for they do not know that they are doing evil. Be not rash with your mouth, nor let your heart be hasty to utter a word before God, for God is in heaven and you are on earth. Therefore let your words be few.* (Eccles. 5:1-2)

RULE #2 – PRAISE MORE

Biblical prayers are full of praise, enhancing worshipful communion with God. Our prayers are full of petitions, treating God like he's management and we're the union grievance representative. But what is praise and how do we do it?

Ever been around Christians that punctuated their sentences with "Praise the Lord!" I hope you do not think me unspiritual, but such people make me want to vomit. Whatever else is going on, I can guarantee they do *not* understand praise. Saying, "Praise the Lord!" is no more praising God than saying, "Love your wife" is deepening your marriage. That phrase is simply a command to do it; it is a command to someone else to praise the Lord. No actual praising of the Lord occurs.

Praise is a worshipful confession to God of who he is and what he does. Praising God centers on a declaration of the attributes of God. We praise his grace, mercy, love, justice, holiness, eternity and sovereignty. We say back to God who he is and what he does in a personal way. We talk to him and say, for example, "You are holy and righteous." That's praising God. To just make a statement to someone else that God has attributes of holiness and righteousness is true, but it's not praise. Praise is addressed to God alone.

Praise is also not thanksgiving, though I'm convinced few Christians understand that. I recall a lot of prayer meetings where the leader says, "Let's begin by spending a few minutes praising God." Then what immediately follows is not praising God, but *thanking* God – two very different things! It's the difference between saying to your wife or husband, "I love you. You're wonderful" versus "Thanks for taking out the garbage." It makes a big difference!

Understand that we are also called to give thanks to God throughout the Scripture, but don't confuse thanks with praise. Most Christians practice thanking God, and that's good, though limited. Praise is the highest form of communication with God. It is the ultimate of relational prayer.

RULE #3 – PETITION LESS

The more we praise God, the less we feel the need to petition him. The more intimate we are with God, the less we feel the need to ask him for things. I think praise draws us into the reality of Christ's statement in Matthew 6:8:

" . . . *your Father knows what you need before you*

ask him."

It's also true that when we talk less in prayer, we are automatically petitioning less.

Let's go back to the father-child relationship. Do your children ask for every need that comes to their mind? Do they say to their father:

> *Don't forget to buy groceries.*
> *Please pay the utility bill.*
> *Did you lock the door?*
> *Be sure to drive carefully!*

Your kids don't say those things because they know you are taking care of them. They *presume* their basic needs are provided. But why would they make that presumption? **Isn't it because of their relationship with their father?** Based on years of relating to their father, they know those basic needs will be provided. They know he's taking care of them. Jesus declares this same spiritual truth in Matthew 6:31-33:

> *Therefore do not be anxious, saying, "What shall we eat?" or "What shall we drink?" or "What shall we wear?" For the Gentiles seek after all these things, and your heavenly Father knows that you need them all. But seek first the kingdom of God and his righteousness, and all these things will be added to you.*

The more intimate you are with God, the less need you feel to ask him for things. Thus, we are back to the concept of Relational Prayer. We focus on knowing him as our true Father and cultivating that love relationship. We still petition

God, but a lot less. His presence and care simply keep us too busy to concern ourselves with asking for things.

RULE #4 – MEDITATE MORE

Meditation grows out of the points we've been discussing – more listening, more praising and less petitioning. Like praise, meditation is often mentioned in the Bible, but seldom practiced by contemporary Christians. I know of nothing that will teach you biblical meditation the way a Personal Retreat will. Meditation is almost automatic on a retreat, and it's almost impossible in our usual frenzied routines. J. I. Packer notes:

> . . . *meditation is a lost art today, and Christian people suffer grievously from their ignorance of the practice. Meditation is the activity of calling to mind, and thinking over, and dwelling on, and applying to oneself, the various things that one knows about the works and ways and purposes and promises of God. It is an activity of holy thought, consciously performed in the presence of God, under the eye of God, by the help of God, as a means of communion with God.*[8]

Meditation, like praise, focuses on who God is and what he has done. Scriptural meditation thus has an object, while non-Christian, Eastern religion meditation does not. It typically focuses on nothingness. We have something far superior to saying a big "ommmmmmmmmmmmmmmmmm" for meditation. We meditate not to empty our minds, but to transform our hearts.

Meditation is the unhurried contemplation and reflection upon the truth of God and his word. Charles Spurgeon put it this way:

There are times when solitude is better than company and silence is wiser than speech. We would be better Christians if we were alone more often, waiting on God and gathering, through meditation on His Word, spiritual strength for His service. We are spiritually fed when we think on the things of God. Truth is like a cluster of grapes. If we want wine we must bruise, press, and squeeze it many times. The bruiser's feet must come down joyfully on the grapes, or else the juice will not flow. They must tread the grapes well, or else much of the precious liquid will be wasted. So must we by meditation tread the clusters of truth if we would get the wine of consolation.[9]

Meditation parallels rumination – the act of a ruminant chewing its cud. To properly understand biblical meditation we have to first understand cud chewing. Ruminants like cows, goats and sheep have four stomachs – the reticulum, rumen, omasum and abomasum. The process begins with chewing. A cow, for example, will make 40,000 – 60,000 jaw movements per day. That's a lot of chewing! That chewed food initially goes into a "fermentation vat," the first part of which is called the reticulum. The honeycombed structure of the reticulum helps bring boluses of food back up for further chewing (chewing the cud), as well as catching heavy foreign objects that are rejected from the digestive process.

The cud then goes to the second part of the fermentation vat, the rumen. Using strong contractions the rumen acts as a mixing chamber. It maintains an environment for 500 trillion digestive bacteria and 50 billion protozoa. These beneficial organisms synthesize nutrients including protein and B vitamins. In addition the rumen removes waste products.

Absorption of nutrients begins with the next "stomach," the omasum. Likened to pages of a book, the numerous surfaces of the omassum absorb fatty acids and electrolytes.

Finally the food reaches the true stomach, the abomasum. It again contains many page-like leaves for absorption of nutrients. As with a human stomach, the abomasums secretes hydrochloric acid and enzymes to break down proteins. The ruminant's digestive process concludes, like our own, with the small intestine and large intestine. Through his creation God has thus given us a picture of biblical meditation – chewing, purifying, fermenting, breaking down the hard to digest and absorbing.

I learned more about meditation from watching cows and goats chew their cud than from any other source. My wife and I spent the summer of 1976 in her grandparents second home along the Wilson River in the dairy country of Tillamook, Oregon while writing my first book. From our kitchen table I would look out on the cows grazing and then chewing their cud in the adjacent pasture. The more I watched them, the more fascinated I became with the sheer amount of time they spent at cud chewing. But another thing impressed me: they were so relaxed and unhurried. It relaxed me to watch them. By instinct those cows knew this behavior was essential to survival. Through that model I learned the similar necessity of meditating on God and his word. To not meditate, to not chew our spiritual cud, leads to spiritual indigestion and spiritual nutrient deficiencies.

Meditation takes time, which is probably the main reason we don't do it. One of the reasons a Personal Retreat lends itself to meditation is simply that you for once have the *time* to meditate. Being an unhurried activity, meditation easily flows from a retreat time. You will discover that meditation is almost automatic on a Personal Retreat.

EXAMPLE OF THE PSALMS

The Psalms exemplify this different way to pray. For example, Psalm 131 strongly shows us Relational Prayer:

O Lord, my heart is not lifted up; my eyes are not raised too high; I do not occupy myself with things too great and too marvelous for me. But I have calmed and quieted my soul, like a weaned child with its mother, like a weaned child is my soul within me. (Ps. 131:1-2)

Many Psalms exemplify praise. Take the opening of Psalm 8:

O Lord, our Lord, how majestic is your name in all the earth! You have set your glory above the heavens. (Ps. 8:1)

Psalm 145 is a personal favorite as a model for praising God. Note that the Psalm begins with the *promise* to praise God, not with actual praise itself:

*I **will** extol you, my God and King, and bless your name forever and ever. Every day I **will** bless you and praise your name forever and ever.* (Ps. 145:1-2)

The real praise doesn't begin in earnest until later:

The Lord is gracious and merciful, slow to anger and abounding in steadfast love. The Lord is good to all, and his mercy is over all that he has made. (Ps. 145:8-9)

What about thanksgiving? Psalm 9 provides a great example of thanksgiving combined with praise. I would note that praise far outshines thanksgiving in the Psalm:

I will give thanks to the Lord with my whole heart; I will recount all of your wonderful deeds . . . But the Lord sits enthroned forever; he has established his throne for justice, and he judges the world with righteousness; he judges the peoples with uprightness. The Lord is a stronghold for the oppressed, a stronghold in times of trouble. (Ps. 9:1, 7-9)

How about petition in the context of Relational Prayer? We might turn to Psalm 31:

In you, O Lord, do I take refuge; let me never be put to shame; in your righteousness deliver me! Incline your ear to me; rescue me speedily! Be a rock of refuge for me, a strong fortress to save me! For you are my rock and my fortress; and for your name's sake you lead me and guide me; you take me out of the net they have hidden for me, for you are my refuge. Into your hand I commit my spirit; you have redeemed me, O Lord, faithful God. (Ps. 31:1-5)

When you read the Psalms, do they sound like the way you pray? That's the key question. Let them teach you a different way to pray.

Every Christian knows prayer is important. The question is, "How are you doing at prayer?" Has Jesus taught you to pray, as he did the disciples? I don't know about you, but I feel like he's only just begun to teach me to pray. Unfortunately, our Christian culture has taught us what is in many cases the wrong way to pray. We've learned to pray like a child presenting Santa a Christmas list instead of using prayer to come into deep relationship with God. Prayer is foundational to encountering God. To really pray is to commit oneself to a lifelong learning and discipline process. But what joy results from that intimate communion.

Personal Retreats both require this different kind of prayer as well as teaching you this kind of prayer. To commit to spending a period of time alone seeking God, reading his word, journaling, etc. will move you into this different kind of prayer, a kind of prayer that characterizes an intimate relationship with God. But how can we further intensify our communication with God? Let's look next at fasting.

FOR FURTHER THOUGHT & DISCUSSION

1. How important is prayer to you?

2. How satisfied are you with your prayer life?

3. Discuss the statement, "You need to shut up more when you pray."

4. Are your prayers more like presenting Santa Claus a Christmas list or just spending time talking with your closest friend?

5. Why do most people focus their prayer life on asking for things rather than praise?

6. How would you describe the difference between biblical meditation and eastern religion meditation?

Chapter Eight

Should I Fast?

What about fasting during your "face to face" time alone with God? Is that part of the process? How does fasting fit in? Maybe a better question to ask is, "What about fasting period?" Let's first establish the basis of fasting overall before applying it to Personal Retreats.

I studied fasting as a relatively new Christian, having been fascinated by both the physical and spiritual benefits. During my second year of college campus ministry, reading *God's Chosen Fast* by Arthur Wallis[1] particularly moved me. A lot of my interest resulted from being assigned the task of presenting a message on fasting at a Campus Crusade for Christ Christmas Conference in Salt Lake City. A few days before going to that event, I recall sharing about it with my home church pastor in Portland. He remarked about how fasting *used* to be practiced by Christians. Arthur Wallis notes:

> *For nearly a century and a half fasting has been out of vogue, at least in the churches of the West. The very idea of someone actually fasting today seems strange to most twentieth-century Christians. They associate it with mediaeval Christianity, or perhaps with High Church practice.*[2]

To my pastor fasting was merely an archaic curiosity of centuries past. He had never considered the biblical basis for fasting, nor its contemporary relevance. Needless to say, he wasn't my pastor for very long after that!

Few Christians fast, whether for physical or spiritual purposes. But should that be any surprise? Like it or not, few Christians seriously seek God. The Church is characterized by far more *professors* of the faith than *possessors* of the faith. Fasting runs counter to our culture of affluence, indulgence and self-gratification. Making something more important than your belly requires a degree of commitment.

A BIBLICAL DISCIPLINE

Even the most cursory reading of the Bible discovers repeated instances of fasting. Here are only a few of the many Old Testament examples we might cite:

Eliezer seeking a bride for Isaac (Gen. 24:33)

Moses on Mt. Sinai (Exod. 34:28)

Hannah praying for a child (1 Sam. 1:7-8)

David upon hearing of Saul's death (2 Sam. 1:12)

David upon hearing of Abner's death (2 Sam. 3:35)

David while praying for God to spare Bathsheba's child (2 Sam. 12:16-23)

Elijah en route to Horeb (1 Kings 19:8)

Jehoshaphat before battle (2 Chron. 20:3)

Ezra mourning the faithlessness of the returning exiles (Ezra 9:5; 10:6)

Nehemiah for the restoration of Jerusalem (Neh. 1:4)

Returned exiles in Jerusalem confessing their sin (Neh. 9:1)

Esther before going to the King (Esther 4:16)

Daniel praying for Jerusalem (Dan. 9:3)

Ninevites response to Jonah's preaching (Jon. 3:5-9)

But fasting continues in the New Testament as well:

Jesus' forty day fast during his temptation (Matt. 4:2)

Practiced by John the Baptist (Matt. 9:14-15)

Anna in the temple (Luke 2:37)

Saul at his conversion (Acts 9:9)

Prophets and teachers in Antioch (Acts 13:2-3)

At the appointment of Elders in the churches (Acts 14:23)

Again, these are only a few of the references in Scripture to fasting. Fasting is simply a part of the normal Christian life.

JESUS' INSTRUCTION

Jesus referred to fasting in the Sermon on the Mount:

*And **when** you fast, do not look gloomy like the hypocrites, for they disfigure their faces that their fasting may be seen by others. Truly, I say to you, they have received their reward. But **when** you fast, anoint your head and wash your face, that your fasting may not be seen by others but by your Father who is in secret. And your Father who sees in secret will reward you.* (Matt. 6:16-18) [Emphasis added]

Jesus said **when** you fast, not **if** you fast. Jesus assumes that his followers will fast. His teaching addresses issues of what to do **when** you fast. He rebukes the hypocritical motivation for fasting by the religious leaders of the day, presenting fasting as a private devotion and communion with God. Like most everything else, they had perverted fasting from an opportunity to more deeply experience the presence of God to a pride-filled gimmick for showing off to others.

The issue of fasting also presented a controversy between Jesus and the disciples of John the Baptist:

Then the disciples of John came to him, saying, "Why do we and the Pharisees fast, but your disciples do not fast?" And Jesus said to them, "Can the wedding guests mourn as long as the bridegroom is with them? The days will come when the bridegroom is taken away from them, and then they will fast." (Matt. 9:14-15)

The passage reveals several key points about fasting. First, it was the normal practice of the spiritually minded people of the day. The lack of fasting by Jesus' disciples was thus an oddity and mystery to John's disciples.

The second thing I note from this passage is *mourning* as a motivation for fasting. Jesus said fasting was inappropriate in his physical presence, just as it would be for the wedding party to fast during that joyous occasion. In this we perhaps most clearly see the primary purpose of fasting – to get close to God. Since you couldn't get any closer to God than the disciples were in the physical presence of Jesus, fasting was inappropriate.

The third and key point the passage makes is the *promise* of future fasting by Jesus' disciples. He would not always be physically present with them. Then, he promised, they would indeed fast. The disciples undoubtedly fasted after Jesus was taken away temporarily through the crucifixion and more permanently through the ascension. The discipline of fasting has been used to heighten spiritual awareness and enhance one's communion with the Lord ever since.

THE JEWISH WEDDING

To fully appreciate this passage we really need to understand Jewish wedding customs. We might think it strange that the wedding guests would mourn after the bridegroom leaves, thinking of our own weddings where we experience happiness before, during and after the ceremony. Actually this passage makes reference to the betrothal, not what we would think of as the wedding. The wedding here is actually more of an engagement party, though the marriage was considered legally binding at this point.

The process began with the father of the bridegroom selecting a bride, often via a matchmaker. Once the match was agreed to, the bridegroom would travel from his father's house to the home of his bride to begin the betrothal. In this ceremony each would drink from a cup of wine sealing the covenant. Then the bridegroom would return to his father's house for one year during which he would prepare an addition to the home for the couple to live in. This period concluded with the bridegroom returning at a time not exactly known by the bride to consummate the marriage.

Sound familiar? I hope so. The entire process of the Jewish wedding profoundly parallels the Christian experience from being chosen by God to be the Bride of Christ to his second coming to consummate our union and take us to the place he has been preparing. As the chosen Bride of Christ, we participate in a Jewish wedding ceremony every time we celebrate the Lord's Supper. While the bridegroom was away, the bride exclusively focused on preparing herself for his return and their eventual life together. Apparently from the passage as well as tradition, the bride fasted periodically during this time. In modern Jewish weddings (after a one week rather than one year separation) the bride and groom fast on the wedding day, not breaking the fast until the completion of the ceremony. This fasting was in preparation and anticipation of the coming marriage. So we fast today to deepen our relationship with the Lord.

ISAIAH 58

The Bible contains a whole chapter on fasting, a chapter regrettably unfamiliar to most Christians. Isaiah 58 contrasts true and false fasting, the fasting of men with what Arthur Wallis called "God's chosen fast:"

*Why have we fasted, and you see it not? Why have
we humbled ourselves, and you take no knowledge of
it? Behold in the day of your fast you seek your own
pleasure, and oppress all your workers. Behold, you
fast only to quarrel to fight and to hit with a wicked fist.
Fasting like yours this day will not make your voice
to be heard on high. Is such the fast that I choose,
a day for a person to humble himself? Is it to bow
down his head like a reed, and to spread sackcloth
and ashes under him? Will you call this a fast, and a
day acceptable to the Lord? Is this not the fast that
I choose: to loose the bonds of wickedness, to undo
the straps of the yoke, to let the oppressed go free,
and to break every yoke? Is it not to share your bread
with the hungry and bring the homeless poor into
your house; when you see the naked, to cover him,
and not to hide yourself from your own flesh? Then
shall your light break forth like the dawn, and your
healing shall spring up speedily; your righteousness
shall go before you; the glory of the Lord shall be
your rear guard. Then you shall call, and the Lord
will answer; you shall cry, and he will say, "Here I
am."* (Isa. 58:3-9a)

The passage teaches the following purposes of fasting:

1. **To make your voice heard on high** (v. 4)
2. **To humble yourself** (v. 5)
3. **To break satanic power** (v. 6)
4. **To provide for the hungry** (v. 7)
5. **To deny physical appetites to gain spiritual
   awareness** (v. 7)
6. **To experience healing** (v. 8)

7. To have God answer your prayers (v. 9)

8. To experience God's guidance and strength (v. 11)

Not only are these great objectives, but they are also exactly what we want to happen when you go "face to face" with God on a Personal Retreat.

FASTING ON A PERSONAL RETREAT

Fasting typically enhances a Personal Retreat. Essentially fasting achieves a "jump-start" of sorts, more quickly cutting through the "noise" we discussed in Chapter 5. Fasting can do in hours what can take two or three days to do otherwise. Denying your physical appetite sharpens your spiritual appetite. Thus your communion with the Lord is deepened.

My view of fasting on Personal Retreats varies according to the length of the retreat. On a one day Personal Retreat I often fast. Generally you will get more out of a one-day retreat if you fast, since it accentuates the clearing process. However, there are also times when I don't fast on a one-day retreat for physical or other reasons. Sometimes that's simply a function of the outdoor temperature and whether my body with its limited fat reserves can be warm enough without eating that day. The key will always be to follow God's leading, understanding that it is not set in concrete that you *must* fast.

On a multi-day Personal Retreat I often fast the first day, again as a jump-start for the time. You could fast for the whole retreat if so led. I don't due to some physical limitations that make longer fasts difficult. But that's just me. Keep in mind that most Christians have never fasted for any length of time, much less for three or four days. Thus, being out in the middle of nowhere is not the place to learn. Recognize your limitations by practicing fasting in your normal environment before venturing into the outback without food.

In deciding about fasting on a Personal Retreat consider the weakening and strengthening effects. Most people will initially feel weaker when they fast as their body detoxifies. Some people will feel strengthened after a day or two of fasting. You may feel greatly energized by fasting or just the opposite. If you're too weak from fasting, that may interfere with your objectives for the Personal Retreat. Some moderation in fasting (and most everything else) is helpful, especially if you're new to fasting. I suggest you get some experience with fasting -- experiment. Don't overdo. Above all else, be led by the Holy Spirit.

THE DECISION TO FAST

So how do you really decide whether to fast on a Personal Retreat or at any other time? What does it mean to be led by the Holy Spirit? How can you really know for sure? I don't absolutely know the answer to those questions, at least not for you. However, here are some general suggestions. First, read the scriptural passages on fasting such as Isaiah 58. God primarily speaks to us through his written word. You may thus be impressed to fast on a particular occasion.

Secondly, I suggest some trial and error. If you've never fasted before, I recommend you try it for one day. But experiment before you go on a Personal Retreat so you know what's involved. On your first Personal Retreat, I suggest *not* fasting. You're already dealing with a new experience, so it's best not to set up too many variables. I would suggest trying out fasting on a subsequent retreat.

PHYSICAL EFFECT OF FASTING

Reservations about fasting may develop from not really understanding what happens physically when you fast. Fasting is *not* starving! Fasting is a process wherein your body lives off of reserves. Imagine you were stranded in a cabin in a snowstorm. You would first burn your firewood in the stove or fireplace. When the regular fuel runs out you would start burning junk – newspapers, magazines, etc. Then you might burn books. The last thing you would burn would be more valuable items such as your furniture.

Similarly, fasting shuts off the body from using its regular fuel. It first burns the junk – fat, dead cells, etc. Because there are many toxins stored in those fat cells, fasting has a detoxifying effect on the body, an effect that may make you feel a bit poorly with the elimination of those toxins. Arthur Wallis notes:

> *What of the general physical benefits? This cleansing process usually produces, after a prolonged fast, a brightness of the eye, pure breath, clear skin and a sense of physical well being.[3]*

In addition to physically detoxifying the body, fasting accentuates the mental processes. Processing of food via the digestive organs requires a lot of energy and blood circulation by the body. Think about it: How mentally sharp are you after eating a large meal? But when you fast and let the digestive tract rest, more circulation is available to your brain. If you've never fasted before, you will be amazed at how mentally sharp you become during the process. Wallis comments:

The sense faculties of the body, especially tasting and smelling, tend to be quickened and sharpened, while one's mental powers become remarkably clear and active.[4]

Virtually all religions incorporate fasting, having observed this connection with increased mental awareness. Biblical fasting, of course, involves a lot more than just freeing up more blood for your brain. Though we can acknowledge the often-observed physical and mental benefits of fasting, our primary objective focuses on spiritual benefits.

One of the greatest misconceptions about fasting concerns hunger. You're not really hungry when you're fasting. Initially you feel the sensation of the stomach being empty, but that is not true hunger. After a day or two, that sensation goes away due to a physiologic change in the body. Allan Cott, M.D. notes:

When you eat anything at all, your gastric juices and digestive system remain in a state of stimulation. While you are still digesting the last food you ate, your palate is already looking forward to more food. When you eat nothing at all, your body steps up its production of a compound called ketones. These ketones, which are broken down products of fatty acids, are released into the bloodstream. As they increase in quantity they suppress the appetite.[5]

When you commit to fasting for a period of time, that decision, in and of itself, seems to cancel some of the hunger sensation. Part of what we call "hunger" we might better call "habit." We have programmed ourselves to be hungry three (or more) times per day. Once you've firmly decided not to eat for the day, the natural hunger signal usually dissipates.

One can potentially fast for a month or more. On average it takes forty days before protein metabolism occurs, the point at which your body is breaking down healthy tissue to survive. This is true hunger, the hunger described in the temptation of Jesus:

And Jesus, full of the Holy Spirit, returned from the Jordan and was led by the Spirit in the wilderness for forty days, being tempted by the devil. And he ate nothing during those days. And when they were ended, he was hungry.
(Luke 4:1-2)

At the end of the forty days, Jesus was experiencing true hunger – the breakdown of healthy tissues. Obviously this "real" hunger is way beyond the scope of our interest in relatively short fasts on Personal Retreats.

WHO SHOULD NOT FAST

For most people fasting is perfectly safe and healthy, but there are a few exceptions. If you are thin (I know from experience) you may not handle longer fasts well, particularly during the cooler times of the year. However, one-day fasts seldom pose a problem. Generally fasting should be avoided if you're pregnant, if you have diabetes, or if you have any other serious health problem. That's not to say it's impossible to fast with serious health problems, but merely that you shouldn't do it on your own. Actually, fasting can be very healing for a lot of health problems. In fact there's an old German proverb that says:

The illness that cannot be cured by fasting cannot be cured by anything else.[6]

If in doubt, check it out with a *qualified* health professional, not just any conventional medical doctor. In other words, don't pool your ignorance with a doctor that knows less about fasting than you do, but rather one that actually understands the process.

HOW TO FAST

Instruction on fasting involves a little more than just saying "Don't eat!" The kind of fasting I'm referring to is usually called a "normal fast." That means you eat no food and drink only water. So no juices, vitamins or anything else – just water. There are other forms of fasting that may be done for health reasons, such as juice fasting or restricted diets, but here we're talking about biblical type fasts for spiritual purposes.

A more unusual type of fast that is also found in the Bible is the "absolute fast." After his blinding light conversion, Saul neither ate nor drank for three days (Acts 9:9). While one can perform a normal fast for up to forty days as Jesus did, an absolute fast maximum length is three days. After that you begin to die of thirst. This type of fast is highly atypical and is not recommended due to this high potential for physical damage.

When you fast you need to increase your water intake. Increased detoxification requires increased water to eliminate those toxins. Most people don't drink enough water anyway – much to the detriment of their health. The normal rule of thumb is to drink half your body weight in pounds in ounces of water daily. Thus, a 128-pound person would drink 64 ounces of water per day – two quarts. For fasting I would suggest increasing that water intake guideline by 50-100%.

Drinking some water tends to placate that empty stomach sensation you will feel during the initial stages of fasting.

One other practical tip: Don't drink tap water while fasting (or in your normal routine for that matter). To detoxify the body you need pure water, not water filled with chlorine, fluoride and a host of other toxins. I recommend steam distilled water, though other types of purified water are acceptable.

Rest is an important component of fasting. During a fast part of your normal body energy will be diverted to cleansing and detoxifying functions. That means you will probably feel more tired. So cooperate with the process. Lie down and rest or take a nap. Remember a Personal Retreat is about "being" not "doing." Though it's necessary to rest more while fasting, it's also helpful to have mild exercise like a short, leisurely walk. Avoid strenuous exercise. I often stroll around the area where I'm camped for a Personal Retreat, especially at dusk. Though it's exercise, it's a resting kind of exercise that enhances the retreat experience.

BREAKING A FAST

Virtually all authorities on fasting agree that the most important aspect of a fast is how you break the fast, that is, how you return to normal eating. Breaking a fast the wrong way can easily undo the physical health benefits, not to mention making you feel badly.

A one-day fast is not a big problem to break. At the appointed time to end the fast, I usually just eat a couple pieces of fruit or drink some juice. Then I wait an hour or two before eating something else. The first meal should be light, such as soup or steamed vegetables. Definitely avoid meat or other heavy proteins on that first meal, since your digestive tract is still waking up.

If you are fasting longer than one day, the usual rule of thumb is to spend as many days breaking the fast as you did on the fast. For example, if you fasted for three days you would take three days transitioning back into normal eating, gradually adding more complex foods. Juices and fruits are pretty simple to digest, followed by cooked vegetables, then raw vegetables, then grains and finally protein foods like nuts, dairy products and meats. Breaking the fast actually requires more discipline than the fast itself. During the fast the sensation of hunger has dissipated, but it comes back with full fury once you start eating. Just remember, your digestive system likes to wake up slowly.

Fasting, as a forgotten discipline, continues to be rediscovered by contemporary Christians desperate for a deeper communion with God. When combined with a Personal Retreat, fasting greatly speeds and intensifies the impact of the experience. Fasting helps make the transition from the "noise" of our usual life's routine to the quiet contemplation of a Personal Retreat. Many of my best Personal Retreats have involved fasting, making it a favorite tool for these special times with God.

I would again emphasize that fasting is not essential to a Personal Retreat. Just as I've had many great retreats with fasting, I've also had a lot without fasting. As I discussed, there are many variables that affect the decision to fast or not to fast. I continue to exhort you to simply let God lead you and teach you about fasting. If you've never fasted, try it during your normal life routine. Get some experience and an understanding of what fasting is like, how it feels and what it does for you. Then, when you come to appreciate this discipline, try adding it to a Personal Retreat. I think you will be impressed.

Now we've examined all the pieces of the puzzle of Personal Retreats. So how do we put them together? How do we actually do a Personal Retreat?

FOR FURTHER THOUGHT & DISCUSSION

1. To what extent have you practiced biblical fasting?

2. Why do you think so few Christians today fast, given it is a common practice throughout the Bible?

3. Why did Jesus' disciples not fast like the disciples of John the Baptist?

4. Discuss how the Jewish wedding customs parallel the Christian life – including fasting.

5. Which of the eight purposes for fasting listed in Isaiah 58 have you practiced? Which do you need to practice?

6. How might fasting be best used on a Personal Retreat?

7. Why do you think that fasting is common to all major religions?

8. How would you decide whether or not to fast on a Personal Retreat?

Chapter Nine

Personal Retreat How-To's

Personal Retreats involve planning *and* the leading of the Holy Spirit. Without some planning your retreat will remain unfocused. Without the whole process being Spirit-led you will not really meet with God. I cannot offer a specific template, but rather general guidelines that will help you find your way. I'm sure there are as many methods of personal retreating as there are people pursuing this discipline. You will undoubtedly "customize" your own approach with experience. This chapter will simply show you one approach – my approach to Personal Retreats.

GENESIS OF A PERSONAL RETREAT

What motivates a Personal Retreat? What causes you to say, "I need a Personal Retreat?" I find it to be a combination of **felt need** and **Spirit leading.** A "felt need" results from providential circumstances such as:

1. Suffering.

Save me, O God! For the waters have come up to my neck. (Ps. 69:1)

As discussed in Chapter One, suffering produces thirst. Difficult, painful circumstances form much of the basis of Christian experience. God's wonderful plan for our lives is trouble! Like horses led to water, we choose not to drink. So God feeds us the salt of suffering. You may suffer from problems in your marriage, finances, children, work, church or whatever. Suffer enough and your thirst and desire for God's intervention will grow. Bottom line, we only trust God when we have to. Oswald Chambers wrote:

When God gets us alone by affliction, heartbreak, or temptation, by disappointment, sickness, or by thwarted affection, by a broken friendship, or by a new friendship—when He gets us absolutely alone, and we are dumbfounded, and cannot ask one question, then He begins to expound.[1]

2. Major Decision.

Make me know your ways, O Lord; teach me your paths. Lead me in your truth and teach me, for you are the God of my salvation; for you I wait all the day long. (Ps. 25:4-5)

Often a major life decision will motivate a Personal Retreat. Throughout our lives we must make decisions about relationships, business, employment, residence location, educational plans and the like. The number one question Christians ask is, "How can I know God's will for my life?" Oh, how I have agonized over that question often in the first ten or twenty years of knowing the Lord. Yet today, after many Personal Retreats, it seems such a stupid question. Let me tell you what God's will for your life is: to be in an intimate relationship with him. God's will for your life is simply to let him live his life through you in an unhindered way . . . and that's where Personal Retreats come in.

Discovering God's will in a given situation is not a matter of hearing a "still, small voice" or of some well-meaning friend or evangelist giving you a "word of knowledge." Those are poor, often pathetic substitutes. If you are in union with him, if you are abiding as a branch in Christ as the vine, you will be in his will. As a child, if I wanted to go where my dad was going, all I had to do was stick close to him. If you're close to God, you will automatically be fulfilling his will. Oswald Chambers said:

> *The child of God is not conscious of the will of God because he is the will of God.[2]*

Personal Retreats don't give you a mechanical formula for knowing God's will; they just help you know God – a much superior approach. Again, it's all about being "face to face."

3. Need for Renewal.
> *But he himself went a day's journey into the wilderness and came and sat down under a broom tree. And he asked that he might die, saying, "It is enough; now, O Lord, take away my life, for I am no better than my fathers."* (1 Kings 19:4)

Have you come to the point of exhaustion in your spiritual life, like Elijah? Maybe you've burned the proverbial candle at both ends for too long. Maybe you're just overwhelmed with long and painful suffering. Maybe you just know something is missing that you deeply long for in your relationship with Jesus Christ. This is a great motivation for a Personal Retreat. Let your needs drive you to spend time away and alone with God.

4. Repentance.

And Jacob was left alone. And a man wrestled with him until the breaking of the day . . . So Jacob called the name of the place Peniel, saying, "For I have seen God face to face, and yet my life has been delivered." (Gen. 32:24, 30)

For Jacob a life of lies and deception met God on that lonely night in the desert. His Personal Retreat focused on repentance from a life of self-dependence. Christians get off track. They sometimes fall into overt sins of commission, as well as the more frequent sins of omission. I don't think repentance is as simple as praying a thirty second mechanical prayer of confession (as I've done several thousand times). We need to **repent of our repentance**. Repentance typically requires wrestling with God, just as Jacob wrestled. God doesn't need a prolonged process to forgive and restore, but we do. Without almost a meditation on our sin, an agonizing over our abuse of the grace of God, we don't really get the impact of repentance. Time alone with God, cleared of the noise in our heads, can greatly accentuate this process.

SPIRIT LEADING

And I am sure of this, that he who began a good work in you will bring it to completion at the day of Jesus Christ. (Phil. 1:6)

Just as felt needs drive us to Personal Retreats, so does the Holy Spirit in his never-ending task of leading us into all truth (John 16:13) as he conforms us to the image of Christ (Rom. 8:29). You may say, "God has never called me to a time away with him, to a Personal Retreat." How do you know? Would you know his voice if you heard it? Have you ever cleared the "noise" from your head so you could clearly hear his voice? I am reminded of the story of young Samuel serving Eli in the Temple (1 Sam. 3:4-14). God was speaking to Samuel, but he was not attuned to the hearing of God's voice until Eli instructed him. God is still speaking, but are we hearing him?

Hearing God is the function of a relationship with him. As a child did you ever get lost in a crowd, away from your father? But if he were calling out your name, couldn't you hear his voice in spite of the crowd? Why? Because of **time** in **relationship** you know your father's voice. Jesus described it this way:

My sheep hear my voice, and I know them, and they follow me. (John 10:27)

Now, if you had only spent as much time with your earthly father as many do with their heavenly father, you probably wouldn't recognize Dad's voice across the room, much less across the crowd. The more time you have spent in communicating with God (relational prayer), the better you know his voice. Because of that *cumulative intimacy* he can impress upon you that it's time for a Personal Retreat.

151

But how do you really know for sure? It's like being in love – you just know.

Scripture is clear that God does direct his children to go away to certain places to receive certain messages from him. As discussed in my earlier chapter, Abraham was called to a specific place – Mt. Moriah – to sacrifice Isaac. Why did he have to go all that distance? God always has a purpose. That location would become the site of the altar of sacrifice in Solomon's temple centuries later. Similarly Moses was called to the top of Mt. Sinai. Why didn't God just give Moses the Ten Commandments as he worshipped in the Tabernacle there in the camp? Somehow God values speaking to us in special places, in remote places away from our usual distractions.

Psalm 37 gives us helpful instruction at this point:

Trust in the Lord, and do good; dwell in the land and befriend faithfulness. Delight yourself in the Lord, and he will give you the desires of your heart.
(Ps. 37:3-4)

If you commit your way to the Lord, he will give you the desires of your heart. Why? If you're committed to him, if you're in communion with him, the desires of your heart are the desires of his heart. In other words, desire nothing but God's will and you may then do whatever you please. Is there a place you yearn to go, a place you perhaps have never been to, but always wanted to visit? That desire of your heart may be part of God's leading you to a Personal Retreat.

PERSONAL RETEAT OBJECTIVES

Do we really need "objectives" for a Personal Retreat? Why not just go and meet with the Lord and allow whatever to happen? Let me answer with another question: Why not go duck hunting or deer hunting, but not bother to aim? Shooting without aiming tends to miss the target. It's the same with Personal Retreats. Though your retreat will often go outside your objectives as God speaks to you in unplanned areas, you still benefit from an initial focus.

The overall objective of every Personal Retreat should be to deeply commune with God. However, that doesn't preclude putting forth specific concerns to the Lord; seeking him on those specific questions. Most of those objectives you will clearly know in advance, since they were the reasons for your Personal Retreat. The Lord will often impress you en route to your retreat with yet other objectives. Don't be afraid to think, but keep open to God's leading in the process as well.

Your journal facilitates this structure. I begin a Personal Retreat by defining two to four objectives in my journal. These are essentially questions that I am bringing before God. I number them #1, #2, #3 and so on. Then, as any insights come, I record them in the journal with the notation "1", "2", etc. to identify the question that answer pertains to. I do the same thing with scripture passages.

Your journal will become a rich source of encouragement to you as you review how God spoke to you during your Personal Retreat. A journal allows you to develop your thoughts, meditate upon them and perhaps review your retreat years later when you need that same message again.

FINDING THE TIME

Few people can just leave for a Personal Retreat without advance planning. How do you find the time? You don't –

you make the time! If you don't set aside the time, it will never happen. Let's face it: some "urgent" item will always come up to crowd out a Personal Retreat (or about anything else you should do). Don't plan for some mythical time when you won't be "so busy" and will have "more time" to do a retreat. You are only deluding yourself.

Everyone has the same amount of time – 24 hours per day. Doing a Personal Retreat involves simply setting priorities. Do you want to do this? Then do it! Don't do it "someday." Don't do it "when . . . ." Just do it. Make it a priority. Do it when you're busy – that's probably when you most need it. If you deceive yourself, you're the only one fooled.

I am reminded of a friend that looks with a little envy on the extensive traveling I've done my whole adult life in the outdoors, including to the National Parks. Now this is someone living in the Northwest who has never been to Yellowstone, Glacier, Zion, Bryce Canyon, Arches or most of the other amazing treasures that are the western National Parks. But he told me, "Someday I'd like to get a motor home and just travel around the country visiting all those places." Two problem words here: "someday" and "like" to. He never will; he's just deceiving himself. Something you won't do in the strength of your twenties and thirties you'll never do in your sixties. What do you really want? That's the question of priorities. What do you really want? What you're doing right now, that's what! Personal Retreats demand a radical shift in priorities.

SHORT PERSONAL RETREATS

A Personal Retreat need not be a several day affair. I define a Short Personal Retreat as a one-day (or even half-day), non-overnight retreat. Obviously you can't go very far on a one-day retreat. You just need a reasonably quiet place away from home to spend time talking and listening to God.

Personal Retreats parallel with cleaning your house. A short retreat is like a quick vacuuming, while a long retreat is more like spring-cleaning. Short Personal Retreats can, like vacuuming, serve as "maintenance retreats" in between your multi-day, more intense "spring cleaning" Personal Retreats that are done less often. This shorter time may be focused on a particular felt need or have the more generalized objective of simply spending time with the Lord. A short, one-day retreat won't provide all the benefits of three or four days away, but it will nevertheless be a rich time. In my view it's better to take several one-day Personal Retreats throughout the year than to go too long waiting for that longer retreat that's much harder to schedule.

LONG PERSONAL RETREATS

I love long Personal Retreats, though I'm sometimes limited for months at a time to only doing short retreats. Long retreats, which I define as having at least one overnight, can be simply life changing. So profound can the impact be that I can remember every single long Personal Retreat I've ever done, and through my journals, recall the truths God taught me.

A long retreat can involve significant travel. I usually travel 100 – 400 miles, though you don't have to go that far away to have an effective time. I simply find that I am "set free" by distance from home. The farther I am from home and work, the less "noise" is cluttering my head. There is a certain freedom that comes from being too far away to easily go home for some "urgent" need. The world gets to wait while you and God wrestle in the wilderness.

If you're at all like me, you probably can't do Long Personal Retreats very often – maybe only once or twice per year. You may have to plan far in advance, or you may just learn to seize the opportunity to leave for a few days when you need to. I recommend for adequate "clearing" purposes, as discussed earlier, that you allow at least two full days at your retreat location not counting travel days. Your greatest insights will typically occur a couple of days into your retreat time.

WHERE TO GO

So, where do you go for a Personal Retreat?

Personal Retreats must take you from the man-made world you live in every day to the God-made world of nature. A poem (author unknown) reads:

I wasted an hour one morning beside a mountain stream,

I seized a cloud from the sky above and fashioned myself a dream,

In the hush of the early twilight, far from the haunts of men,

I wasted a summer evening, and fashioned my dream again.

Wasted? Perhaps. Folks say so who never have walked with God,

When lanes are purple with lilacs or yellow with goldenrod.

But I have found strength for my labors in

that one short evening hour.

*I have found joy and contentment; I have
found peace and power.*

*My dreaming has left me a treasure, a hope
that is strong and true.*

*From wasted hours I have built my life and
found my faith anew.*

As Oswald Chambers tells us:

*Nature to a saint is sacramental. If we are children
of God, we have a tremendous treasure in Nature. In
every wind that blows, in every night and day of the
year, in every sign of the sky, in every blossoming
and in every withering of the earth, there is a real
coming of God to us if we will simply use our starved
imagination to realize it.*[3]

A lot of this depends on you. On a Long Personal Retreat
you will probably choose to go someplace special. Maybe
it's somewhere you've always wanted to go, but never
have. Maybe it's a place you've been before that has special
meaning for you. For example, if you came to receive Christ
at a student retreat at the beach (as I did), that area may
have special spiritual significance for you. Or, if you've had
a particularly meaningful Personal Retreat in the past at a
given place, you may be drawn to return there again and
again. Ask yourself right now, "What place has been special
to me in the past?" What first comes to mind? That may be
an excellent location for your Personal Retreat.

Beyond that, it's different strokes for different folks.
Ocean, mountains, lakes, streams, waterfalls, desert and

canyons – all of these locations are great possibilities depending on the individual. Typically the most inspirational places involve high points, mountains or water. Part of this depends on where you live and therefore what your options are. For example, if you live in the Midwest or the Desert Southwest, you're probably not going to an ocean beach for your retreat.

In the biblical examples cited earlier in this book, the Personal Retreats take place in the deserts and mountains of the Middle East. That's what's in the Middle East – deserts and mountains. But what if you live in Iowa or Ohio? No matter where you live, there are special places, even if they're only special to you.

By way of personal example, I live in the Pacific Northwest, where I can choose between mountains, lakes, streams and the ocean. But I've also spent several winters in the desert in the Southwest, where I've had wonderful Personal Retreats amidst cacti as far as the eye can see. I grew up in the flatlands of Illinois and have wondered where I would go there for a Personal Retreat. Numerous possibilities came to mind such as camping or staying in a cabin on a lake. Wherever you live, special places are waiting for you to come on a retreat.

So how "remote" do you go? Again, this is partly a matter of personal preference. A Personal Retreat requires a certain degree of isolation, but you don't have to backpack into your location. An isolated cabin or relatively quiet campsite may be fine. Many states have cabins or yurts you can rent in their state parks. This is a great alternative for those who are uncomfortable with camping or wish to do a Personal

Retreat in colder weather. You want to be mostly alone, but the objective is not to see how uncomfortable you can be. You need to be able to rest and think and write in your journal. If you're spending 90 percent of your time "surviving" your location, there's not a lot of time for doing the real business of meeting with God.

WHERE YOU CAN'T GO

Though there are endless possibilities of locations *for* your Personal Retreat, there are some places you *cannot* go:

1. Your Home – You can't do a retreat in your own home, even if there's no one else there. You must be in an unfamiliar place, not in a place full of distractions.

2. A City – Personal Retreats require quiet and solitude and you just aren't going to get that in a city. However, I would note that in some cities a more remote, quiet location in a park *might* work for a one-day or partial day retreat.

3. "Occupied" Places – Places with too many people around won't work well for a Personal Retreat. Many even beautiful places have just too many people around to realize the quiet and solitude necessary for a retreat. I love the National Parks, but I generally wouldn't go to one for a Personal Retreat, except in a more remote location or out of peak season. I would sooner do a retreat in Central Park in New York than in Yosemite National Park in August – fewer people!

4. Motel Room – No matter where it's located, a motel room just doesn't work for a Personal Retreat. It's too much like your home. You don't want a TV, radio, the usual comforts of home and lots of other people milling around. You need a unique place, and there's nothing unique about a motel room!

CELL PHONES

We must talk about cell phones. You're not going to have much of a Personal Retreat if someone's calling you on your cell phone every ten minutes. If you go to the kind of places I go to for retreats, there's no cell service anyway, so this isn't an issue. But if you are in cell range, you have to turn the thing off. Call in once a day for messages in case there is an emergency situation, but otherwise forget the cell phone and just let family and others know you're unreachable. Believe it or not, the world will not fall apart if you don't answer your cell phone for a few hours.

CLEARING

Nothing is more important on a Personal Retreat than "clearing." I define "clearing" as emptying yourself of your usual thoughts and concerns. It's a "making room" for God. As a Carmelite priest stated:

Where God finds space, He enters.[4]

Clearing is the main reason you must travel away from home for a Personal Retreat. Problems and stresses tend to dissolve a lot after you've driven 100 miles from home. Clearing actually begins en route. The commitment to doing the retreat sets you up for clearing. You have given yourself permission to do nothing but seek God for a period of time. That powerfully dissipates much of your usual mental "noise." By the time you reach your retreat location, a lot of clearing may have already taken place.

Once you're at your retreat location, don't expect to be immediately wowed with the presence of God. "On site" clearing now begins. The best thing to do on arrival is nothing – relax, take a nap, walk around a little, sit and read.

Just enjoy the place. Metaphorically throw your watch away. Allow time to become irrelevant. Assume you have all the time in the world. Don't be in a hurry for anything. Just let it happen, let it flow. You know you're "cleared" when you are really relaxed and start having insights.

FASTING OR NOT?

Should you fast on a Personal Retreat? A retreat can be done with or without fasting, so let me explain the advantages and disadvantages. The greatest advantage of fasting is that it speeds up the "clearing" process. It puts you into a spiritual plane in a few hours as your focus changes from satisfying bodily appetites to seeking the Lord. Fasting works well on one day Personal Retreats, as well as perhaps the first day of a longer retreat. Obviously fasting also simplifies your planning if you're not packing food.

Having stated the above advantages, fasting also produces disadvantages. The physical detoxifying effect (particularly for those eating the typical American junk food diet) may initially interfere with your mental clarity. Fasting for more than a day may also be difficult for people with certain health problems or who are inexperienced in fasting. Meal preparation and eating on a Personal Retreat can be a special experience, particularly if you're camping. It kind of takes you back to basic physical needs. I'm always more appreciative of food on a retreat, though I'm eating very simple things.

Ultimately the decision to fast or not is a matter of how God is leading you. If you don't sense any particular leading, experiment. Try fasting. Try not fasting and compare.

JOURNALING A PERSONAL RETREAT

Though I've discussed journaling in a previous chapter, I want to apply it to our "how-to's" of doing a Personal Retreat. A journal will solidify and memorialize what happened on your retreat. Without a journal, much of God's message to you will soon be forgotten. With a journal you can relive your Personal Retreat and be reminded of its lessons again and again. When you go on vacation, you take pictures to remember and relive the special places you saw. Your journal is essentially a "picture" of your Personal Retreat for remembering and reliving. Beyond that, just the act of writing down your concerns, insights, scriptures, book quotes, prayers, etc. will root them in your mind.

As I referred to earlier in the chapter, start your Personal Retreat by writing your objectives in your journal. Then record insights, scripture passages and the like keyed to your #1, #2, #3, etc. objectives. Write out your own prayers to God based upon those insights. Just be honest and real. Your journal is just between you and God. After awhile, you may find your journal looking more and more like the Book of Psalms. When that happens, you're definitely doing something right.

BIBLE READING & MEDITATION

I cannot overemphasize the importance of spending time in God's Word during a Personal Retreat. That is primarily how God is going to speak to you during this time. The Psalms are a great place to start, especially if you're hurting. The various Psalms express every possible emotional state a human being can experience. Allow the Holy Spirit to anoint and apply particular passages to you and your situation. Look up cross-references or other passages that come to mind. Just milk dry the special passages you find. Follow where the trail leads and journal what you find.

Pastor Rick Warren describes meditation as "focused thinking" saying:

> *When you think about a problem over and over in your mind, that's called worry. When you think about God's Word over and over in your mind, that's meditation. If you know how to worry, you already know how to meditate! You just need to switch your attention from your problems to Bible verses. The more you meditate on God's Word, the less you will have to worry about.[5]*

Meditation pictures a cow or sheep chewing its cud. These animals progressively digest their food via four stomachs. They swallow the food, then burp it up and chew it some more and so on through this complex digestive process. That's what we're admonished to do with God's Word day and night (Ps. 1:2). You don't just swallow it or just chew it a little and swallow it. You keep regurgitating and chewing and swallowing. You take your time, just like that cow out in the pasture. Nothing looks more relaxed and carefree than an animal chewing its cud. To meditate is to immerse yourself in the passage and let it do likewise with you. Take the time to peacefully and patiently digest it.

BOOK READING

Some of my most profound insights on Personal Retreats resulted from reading a Christian book I had brought along. Frankly, I've had some pretty amazing experiences in this regard. A few years ago I planned a Personal Retreat in the Strawberry Mountains of Eastern Oregon. Almost on a whim right before leaving I thought, "Maybe I should take a book with me to read." I glanced at my bookshelf with hundreds of books and "happened" to grab *You Gotta Keep Dancin'* by Tim Hansel. I had never read the book that had been given to me by a former employee several years prior. As I began reading the book that evening at the Strawberry Campground, I was again and again brought to tears at its perfect relevance to what I was going through at that time. Like Hansel, who had been crippled by a fall while climbing in the Sierras, I too was suffering physical pain with six vertebrae smashed from osteoporosis-produced compression fractures. He was mirroring my life. Perhaps the favorite quote I underlined from the book was:

> *Pain is inevitable, but misery is optional. We cannot avoid pain, but we can avoid joy.*[6]

I'm tearing up recalling this again years later. That's how powerful a Personal Retreat can be.

Ironically, I returned to the Strawberry Mountains while writing this chapter. I again just "happened" to pick another book off my shelf to take on the retreat. It was *Men and Women: Enjoying the Difference* by Dr. Larry Crabb.[7] Again, its emphasis on how self-centeredness destroys relationships was exactly God's message for me on that retreat. And, it's all in my journal. When you are seeking God, you will be amazed at how he sovereignly works through the Scripture, a Christian book, experiences or anything else to bring his message to your heart.

WALKING OR HIKING

Walking is a great way to meditate on what God is saying to you during your Personal Retreat. Not only is it physically stimulating, but it spiritually stimulates as well. A good Personal Retreat location has some inviting places to walk, whether it's along a stream or lake, in the mountains or even in the desert. Some of my most memorable one day retreats have been spent at Saguaro National Park outside of Tucson just walking off the trails amidst the 200 year-old giant cacti.

Walking around a little allows you to process the messages God is impressing on your heart. You can't just sit and read and write in your journal the whole time. Again, it's like the cow chewing its cud – eat for a while, then digest. Let it become a relaxed rhythm.

But what about actual hiking? On a longer Personal Retreat, some hiking is fine. On a shorter retreat, hiking tends to get in the way of focused time with God. You have to guard against your Personal Retreat degenerating into a mere hiking trip. Hiking can be great for "clearing" but use a hike not just to get someplace, but also to seek God all along the way. On a three or four day retreat, I may go on one long hike that takes most of the day. Beyond that, I focus on shorter walks, especially just walking around the area where I'm camped.

WHEN TO GO HOME

So when is a Personal Retreat over? When exactly is it time to go home? Your schedule may dictate that, but if your time is more open-ended, this question will come up. My simple answer to this question is that you leave when you're full. You generally come empty to a Personal Retreat; the idea is to leave full. There is only so much you can successfully process in one retreat – you can only hold so much. More time after that point will not produce a lot of fruit.

Another way of looking at the question of when it's over is to leave when you're illumined. When you know God has delivered a message to you that may be the time to go. Of course, on some retreats God delivers a number of messages to you. You don't necessarily have the answers to all of your questions at the end. Some of the objectives you began with may not be met. That's where we come back to the primary objective of all Personal Retreats – to meet with God. If you've done that, you've had a successful retreat no matter how many questions were left unanswered.

CONCLUSION

Above all else remember that a Personal Retreat is ultimately Spirit-led. Different people will do a retreat in different ways, in different places and for different lengths of time. One size definitely does not fit all. Hopefully the principles and guidelines of this chapter give you enough of a picture of a Personal Retreat to get started. You will fill in the specifics as you go. Personal Retreats are a learned discipline, learned by doing. Need to observe a "face to face" encounter with God up close? How about coming along via my Journal on a past Personal Retreat?

FOR FURTHER THOUGHT & DISCUSSION

1. Describe any tension you feel between planning a Personal Retreat and just being led by the Holy Spirit throughout the process.

2. What "felt needs" are you experiencing right now that a Personal Retreat might address?

3. Have you ever felt led by the Holy Spirit to have a time away with God? How did you know you were being led by the Spirit?

4. Why would God lead believers to particular locations for a "face to face" meeting?

5. Are you feeling led to go on either a short or long Personal Retreat? Which? Why?

6. Discuss the Oswald Chambers statement that "Nature to a saint is sacramental."

Chapter Ten

Journal of a Personal Retreat

I was once told that truth is better "caught" than "taught." In this book we've looked at many aspects of having a special meeting with God: definition, motivation, biblical examples, prayer, fasting and specific how-tos. Yet all of that can be just words on paper if you don't "catch" the vision at the heart level of what a Personal Retreat really is. With that in mind I'm going to attempt to let you eavesdrop on one of my Personal Retreats via my Journal. That is, of course, a little intimidating due to the intensely personal nature of a journal as we discussed in Chapter 6. But I don't know a better way to truly introduce you and hopefully thoroughly infect you with the concept of Personal Retreats.

MY STORY

Before we go on that retreat together, I need to tell you more about my life and the primary struggle that drove me to Personal Retreats. The experience of Personal Retreats comes packaged in a context of life experiences. Therefore to understand what happens on a retreat with a given person, you need to understand something of their life.

No event in my life drove me to spend time on Personal Retreats like a letter I received in August 2003 demanding that I pay a "shakedown" of $1 million and go out of business in the State of Washington. It wasn't a letter from the Mafia, though it might as well have been. It was a letter from the Washington Attorney General's office falsely accusing me of violating the state's Consumer Protection Act in the advertising of my Bellevue and Spokane, Washington nutritional clinics. What followed was a lawsuit, months of depositions, a Summary Judgment against me proscribing a shutdown of my practice and $2 million in penalties, over $400,000 in attorney fees and finally the Washington Court of Appeals partially reversing the ruling and awarding me attorney fees. I was ultimately vindicated.

So what led up to this? I began my adult life in Christian ministry on college campuses. During that time I developed a serious cancer condition and had my health destroyed by conventional cancer treatment. I discovered nutritional approaches to degenerative diseases through another doctor, solved my cancer problem and restored my health. Then, of course, I wanted to tell the world about it, so I started writing books about health and nutrition from a biblical perspective and teaching seminars in churches.

Wanting to more directly help people to better health, in 1984 I completed an unaccredited Ph.D. (though recognized everywhere in the world except the State of Oregon, where I live) in Nutrition and Wholistic Health Sciences and began a nutritional clinic. After struggling a couple of years practicing in Oregon, I moved to the Seattle area, where I eventually discovered a wildly successful marketing approach for our practice – the Free **SICK & TIRED SEMINAR**ˢᴹ, a three hour presentation showing a radically different approach to solving common health problems. In eighteen years I presented over 250 seminars to over 20,000 attendees and had clinics operating in several locations throughout the Northwest with thousands becoming clients. In addition to the seminars I also presented a weekly Christian radio program throughout the Northwest.

So what was the problem? In a word: bureaucrats. None of our clients were complaining—it was just the bureaucrats. The "system" is at war with natural medicine practitioners who threaten the highly profitable status quo the conventional medicine-drug establishment enjoys. State departments of health and attorney general's offices have been infiltrated with bureaucrats committed to protecting the medical monopoly. Thus, most natural medicine practitioners survive by staying "under the radar" – you don't have a problem until they notice you. But once they do notice you, look out!

Prolonged suffering? You have no idea! To say that five years of my life was like having your tonsils taken out through your rectum would be putting it mildly. But what about God? What about the sovereignty of God? Whether I theologically believed God caused this situation or just allowed it, there was no doubt that he could have prevented it. He didn't. His design entailed these years of seemingly endless suffering to one ultimate end – that I would know him. Now that you know a little more about my life, let's go on a Personal Retreat.

STEENS MOUNTAIN PERSONAL RETREAT

As noted in the previous chapter, there are places that become special – places you love to go back to for Personal Retreats. One such place for me is Steens Mountain in Southeastern Oregon. Few places in the lower 48 states are more remote and unknown than this small mountain range located sixty miles south of the small town of Burns. Steens Mountain is a thirty mile long fault block rising to almost 10,000 feet. Its western approach is so gradual one hardly comprehends it as a mountain range. But gazing over the 5000' sheer drop on the eastern side eliminates all doubt about this ruggedly beautiful spot once only occupied by Basque sheepherders. Combining U-shaped glacial valleys, aspen stands, cirque lakes and miles of meadows covered with wildflowers, it's quite unlike anyplace else in the Pacific Northwest, if not in the whole country. It's just totally different.

My family first went to Steens Mountain over twenty years ago out of curiosity. Snow closures still in early summer prevented going up the road to the top, a road that is the highest automobile road in the Pacific Northwest. The next year mechanical problems with our car again prevented us from getting more than a mile or so up the mountain road. It was almost as if some force was preventing us from seeing this special treasure of God's creation. Thanks to some "good Samaritan" cowboys headed into town on a Friday night, we discovered our problem was a clogged fuel filter, got it fixed and finally went up the mountain the next day. I've returned many times since – once for a Personal Retreat.

The following entries in italics are taken directly from my Journal of that retreat. I've indented the entries that were quotes from books or scripture. Bracketed comments are explanations I've added for this writing.

7/27/03 – *Personal Retreat Day #1*

I leave in a few minutes for my Personal Retreat at Steen's Mountain. [This was a 200-mile drive from home in Central Oregon]. *Am now at Fish Lake Campground, only slightly marred by three motor homes 100 yards away that are traveling together. I expect to find quiet, isolated spots all over the mountain to spend time in thought and prayer. I have several objectives for this Personal Retreat:*

#1 – I have come to realize that I don't operate with an awareness of God being so close to me every moment and desirous of being involved in every aspect of my life. I have become a practical deist in many ways – I know God is the source of my life and salvation, but I feel like he's distant and I'm on my own. I know he wants to be my best friend and wants to walk with me as I walk with him.

*#2 – I have lost my heart. This is my main reason for being here. I've come to realize through John Eldredge's books that my heart has gotten buried or lost somewhere. I've spent 35 years as a Christian filling my **mind** with God's truth, only to now realize it belonged also (and primarily) in my heart. God wants to relate to me on the heart level – this is probably the reason for #1 – why I don't sense God's closeness. I've gone through four years of devastating circumstances – I believe all to the end that I might discover God afresh.*

#3 – God, who am I? What do you think of me? What is my real name? [Questions taken from *Waking the Dead* by John Eldredge;[1] the primary book I read during this Personal Retreat, along with rereading one of Eldredge's other books, *Wild at Heart.*]

#4 – What am I to do with the specific financial crises I'm facing? Is Pacific Health Center [my nutritional clinic practice] *to continue? Am I getting other direction?*

#5 – Am I to write more books? That gift is there, and I feel badly for not using it. What and how? [If you're reading this book, you know how that came out!]

#6 – Love. I am lacking in love, which makes sense, since love comes from the heart. Love is not just the commitment of the will toward someone as I have so often thought, based on the Bible's tie in of love with obedience (John 15). **I have been loving with my mind**, *but love must come from the heart. I can't love from my heart because I have lost my heart.*

"Everything you love is what makes life worth living."[2]

[At this point I have laid out my concerns before the Lord – the areas in which I am seeking his ministry in my life. What follows are entries tied back to those initial questions using the same number.]

#2 – "God loves you; you matter to him. That is a fact, stated as a proposition . . . why then aren't we the happiest people of earth? It hasn't reached our hearts. Facts stay lodged in the mind . . . They don't speak at the level we need to hear. Proposition speaks to the mind, but when you tell a story, you speak to the heart."[3]

#6 – What Do I love?
  1. Scenic, remote places
  2. Snow-capped mountain views
  3. Waterfalls
  4. Beaches on the Big Island of Hawaii
  5. Snorkeling
  6. Thunderstorms
  7. Sunrises
  8. The light of a clear, dry morning
  9. Freeing people from health bondages
  10. Persuading people to God's truth via writing or speaking

Major thunderstorm Sunday evening. Now it has blown past and a lovely, refreshing wind is blowing through the aspens. It is a special place.

7/28/03 – Personal Retreat Day #2

The morning is special. Hiking around I realize I could have camped at Pate Lake [a smaller lake about a quarter mile from my campsite] *by myself (with no facilities), but there is something to be said for having an outhouse and a water supply. I plan to spend time during the day there – doesn't matter where I eat dinner and sleep.*

"For not from the east, nor from the west, nor from the desert comes exaltation; but God is the judge; he puts down one, and exalts another." (Psalm 75:6-7)

"God has a storehouse of blessings that He has reserved for you and me. However, our timing to receive those blessings may not be the same as our Lord's. God has a specific timetable that He requires

to accomplish His purposes in the life of the believer.
Sometimes that timetable seems excruciatingly cruel
and painful, yet it is needful . . . If you are awaiting
the fulfillment of a vision in your life, ask the Lord for
His grace to sustain you. It will be worth the wait."[4]

Big Indian Gorge overlook at the end of the road – about
9700'. The cumulus clouds are so huge from this mountaintop.
Temperatures are managing to stay in the seventies so far. A
little snow still remains below the ridges.

#4 – It occurs to me here, experiencing this time of
closeness to God and insights from God, that my will is
much more open to His will. There's sort of a pre-Fall edenic
quality to the experience. I think of a number of things that
I don't really want to do that right now I would be willing
to do . . .

"The heart is the connecting point, the meeting place
between any two persons. The kind of soul intimacy
we crave with God and with others can be experienced
only from the heart. We don't want to be someone's
project; we want to be the desire of their heart . . .
We've done the same to our relationship with God.
Christians have spent their whole lives mastering all
sorts of principles, done their duty, carried on the
program of their church . . . and never known God
intimately, heart to heart."[5]

"My heart is me. The real me. Your heart is you. The
deepest, truest you. That is why the heart is central,
for what shall we do if we dismiss our self?"[6]

What does it really mean to walk with God? One thing it means is that I don't just make decisions based on reason, expedience and practicality. It means sometimes I'm going to be led contrary to what is reasonable . . . God has been teaching me about my heart for a long time – long before I heard of John Eldredge – I just didn't realize it. "Heart" needs have led me to doing Personal Retreats. Heart needs have led me to travel to scenic places.

#3 – Who am I? I am an explorer, an innovator, an entrepreneur, an adventurer.

[This insight finally came after asking the question at the beginning of the retreat. I had never really previously thought about who I was, who God created me to be.]

*I've reached that awkward part of a Personal Retreat when I've gotten **some** insights, I'm feeling alone, and would just like to cut it short. But I know God has more to say to me, if I will just take the time and let Him do His work. I'm thinking about going down the mountain to get ice and go in the 4WD road from the north into McCoy Canyon. I don't really want to stay here – it's gotten too familiar. I did about all the sightseeing I could do on the mountain today. If the temperatures below weren't so hot* [during my retreat cities across the Pacific Northwest experienced highly unusual 100+ degree heat]*, I would go somewhere else for tomorrow night. I'm thankful it is cool here. I do wish the sleeping were easier.*

[I find that part of capturing the experience of a Personal Retreat involves journaling a lot of fairly innocuous thoughts like those above. Part of the experience of the retreat, though, is the discovery that nothing about my thoughts, nothing about my life is insignificant to God. By this point in the retreat it seems as natural to talk with God about the weather as some "spiritual" topic. True intimacy with God, among other things involves dissolution of the false "sacred-secular" dichotomy that unfortunately most Christians operate with.]

"This is written so deeply on our hearts: You must not go alone."[7]

I have gone it alone my whole life and suffered unnecessary defeat as a result. Mostly I've gone it alone because there was no one to go with me. I think [my church] holds more promise than any fellowship I've ever been in. I think there are actually people in the Sunday School class that genuinely care about me.

I must have a small group that will fight for my heart.

"His [Jesus] wildness was in His refusal – or His inability – to live within other's expectations."[8]

I am like that some, but I need to feel freer to be wild in pursuit of God's calling on my life.

I think back to all the sermons I've preached – preached from the mind to the mind. No wonder there was so little fruit. How different it would be now if God should put me in that situation again.

7/29/03 – Personal Retreat Day #3

Slept a lot better – maybe the extra inflation on the air mattress helped.

"You almost have to hold back your natural gifting to insure that God is the one who is guiding you. If not, you will not know if it is through your skill versus His hand that you are accomplishing the work."[8]

So is Pacific Health Center a reflection of my natural gifting, or is it a demonstration of God's work? What could I do differently to allow God's hand to be predominant?

"You are never a great man when you have more mind than heart." – Beauchene[9]

That's been my problem my whole life! I was always the brain – always the mind.

I don't think I ever realized the significance of the Israelites being led by a cloud in the desert. The cloud was covering them, protecting them from the sun. As I sit here at East Rim at 9700' shielded by a large cloud from today's record temperatures, I understand. At least I'm not down below where the temperatures are breaking 100 degrees all over the state, even 100 degrees in Portland. It's a nice 75 or so here. To be led by God is to walk in the shade. [One of the truly amazing aspects of Personal Retreats are the spiritual lessons learned from the observation of nature. Some of my most profound experiences in this regard occurred in Saguaro National Park outside of Tucson, Arizona, where I've had many one-day Personal Retreats. I would observe that after some time of clearing and beginning to get in touch with God, the birds would approach me. Increasing my oneness with God kind of produces a slightly edenic oneness with his creation as well.]

" . . . God delights in being a part of our lives. Do you now why he often doesn't answer prayer right away? Because he wants to talk to us, and sometimes that's the only way to get us to stay and <u>talk</u> to him. His heart is for relationship, for shared adventure to the core."[10]

"The tragedy of life is what dies inside a man while he lives."
– Albert Schweitzer[11]

"Every man repeats the sin of Adam every day. We won't risk, we won't fight, and we won't rescue Eve."[12]

"God thwarts us to save us. We think it will destroy us, but the opposite is true – we must be saved from what really will destroy us."[13]

"The true test of a man, the beginning of his redemption, actually starts when he can no longer rely on what he's used all his life. The real journey begins when the false self fails."[14]

These above relate to Question #4 I think. God is thwarting my efforts, saving me from my false self. What is my false self? Maybe my whole Pacific Health Center character.

What a delight it is to lie on the ground here on this 9700' mountaintop and just gaze at the clouds above. What an amazing place!

#3 – This "name" thing has really grabbed me. Knowing my true name determines in large part who I am and, to a degree, what God thinks of me. There are numerous passages referring to names being written in the Book of Life. Revelation 13:8 adds that my name was written before the foundation of the world. That means I had a name before the world was created – and it's pretty certain it wasn't "Monte." So, what was it? What is it? God gave His true name to Abram (Abraham), Jacob (Israel), Simon (Peter) . . . the name change reflected who they really were – what they

were really to become, which was not apparent at the time of the renaming.

Upon returning to camp I again felt a wave of fear and loneliness to be back home – a sensation I have learned to ignore as not being from God. It usually means, I'm convinced that God has something special for me yet to get at Steens Mountain before leaving in the morning.

"We let God love us; we let him get real close to us . . . few men are ever so vulnerable as to simply let themselves be loved by God." [14]

This hits home. I have too often agreed with the Enemy that I'm no good – how could I have done so many stupid things over the years, how could I have lost so much money, how could I have been such a poor provider to my wife, etc. Those thoughts pop up all of a sudden from guess where? But God simply wants me to let him love me – he wants to bind up my wounds and set the prisoner free.

#3 – He sees me as his battered and bruised child in need of caressing, comforting, healing. Jesus, I release myself, my heart to your love.

The wound clearly goes back to my own father who focused on physical provision – work was the center of his life – but who generally wasn't there with encouragement, who never quite appreciated my dissimilarity, who verbally wounded me so many times . . .

For the first time I understand why I am highly driven, why I never let anyone get close to me – including my wife – and why I am an imposter to most people.

" . . . forgiveness is setting a prisoner free and then discovering the prisoner was you."[14]

"When God looks at you He does not see your sin. He has not one condemning thought toward you (Romans 8:1). But that's not all. You have a new heart. That's the promise of the new covenant: 'I will give you a new heart and put a new spirit in you. I will remove from you your heart of stone and give you a heart of flesh.' (Ezek. 36:26-27) . . . There's a reason it's called good news."[15]

I am excited and fearful to go home. Excited to share and practice what God has taught me – fearful of the inevitable rejection that comes with facing those who have not been to the mountain.

I ponder the quote: "Don't ask yourself what the world needs. Ask yourself what makes you come alive, and go do that, because the world needs people who have come alive."[16]

Does Pacific Health Center make me come alive? Apparently not, since I've worked hard to get out of working there in person. What does make me come alive then?

1. Sharing at Sunday School class or Men's Bible Study.

2. Writing.

3. Speaking – my Sick & Tired Seminars still turn me on.

4. Doing my radio program.

5. Hiking.

This is huge. The move out of Seattle [We moved from Seattle to Central Oregon the previous summer resulting in no small financial hardship and lots of second-guessing.] *was consistent with my heart. Fear is keeping me out from a writing and speaking ministry.*

7/30/03 – Personal Retreat Day #4

"Will the Lord reject forever? And will He never be favorable again? Has His lovingkindness ceased forever? Has His promise come to an end forever? Has God forgotten to be gracious? Or has He in anger withdrawn His compassion? Then I said, 'It is my grief, that the right hand of the Most High has changed.' I shall remember the deeds of the Lord; surely I will remember Thy wonders of old."
--Psalm 77:7-11 (NASB)

*"If you had permission to do what you really want to do, what would you do? Don't ask **how**; that will cut your desire off at the knees. **How** is never the right question; **how** is a faithless question. It means, 'unless I can see my way clearly I won't believe it, won't venture forth.'"*[17]

That's why I left Illinois and came to Oregon. [I grew up in Illinois and fulfilled a dream of moving to Oregon when I started college at age 17.] *What I really want to do is probably not Pacific Health Center. I would rather be writing books, speaking, doing the radio program, traveling and tending the ranch. I chose security over freedom in the ensuing success after the first SICK & TIRED SEMINAR* [November 1988, 260 seminars ago]. *Not that those early days of Pacific Health Center weren't an adventure and not that I didn't very much want that clinical success. I did, but I've grown tired of just making a living while my greater gifts and desires within are being suppressed.*

As the sun has just risen a gentle breeze blows on the aspen. What a unique, unusual and utterly relaxing sound it is.

That was my final entry for the Steens Mountain Personal Retreat of July 2003. As often happens, rereading (and rewriting) my journal stuns me. I had insights on that Personal Retreat that I did not act on until now – years later. But God is faithful and just keeps teaching the lesson until we get it. You can experience more spiritual growth on one Personal Retreat than many Christians do during their entire life.

To be so candid, to let you into a very private four days of my life, is a little painful. But it's also healing to me, and hopefully challenging to you. Your Personal Retreats will probably be nothing like mine. This chapter isn't presented as the official way to journal a retreat, but only as one example. Hopefully, reading an actual journal and "traveling" with me to Steens Mountain "fleshes out" the concept of a Personal Retreat a little better. But I promise you: Your own Personal Retreats will be wonderfully and totally unique to you.

FOR FURTHER THOUGHT & DISCUSSION

1. What did you learn about Personal Retreats from reading the journal of one?

2. Do you have a special place to go away and meet with God?

3. How do you see the questions and answers coming together on this Personal Retreat?

4. In what ways do you identify with the experiences in the journal of this Personal Retreat?

Conclusion

You now know what I know about meeting God "face to face" through Personal Retreats. But the real question is not about knowing, but about doing. Are you ready to encounter God through your own Personal Retreat? Are you thirsty with a thirst that only an encounter with God will satisfy? Your own meeting with God – not this book – will be the real story for you about Personal Retreats. There is no substitute for your own personal encounter with God. Charles Spurgeon wrote a century ago:

Believer, you should be thirsting for the living God. You should be longing to climb the hill of the Lord, desiring to see Him face to face. Do not be content with the mists of the valley when the summit awaits you. My soul thirsts to drink deep of the cup reserved for those who reach the mountaintop. I long to bathe my brow in heaven. How pure are the dews of the hills, how fresh is the mountain air, how rich is the food of the lofty dwellers, whose windows look into the New Jerusalem![1]

As wonderful as Personal Retreats are, the most important part of a retreat is coming home. Like Moses, we don't get to stay on Sinai. Like Jesus we must travel to our Jerusalem. Oswald Chambers wrote:

We have all had times on the mount, when we have seen things from God's standpoint and have wanted to stay there; but God will never allow us to stay there. The test of our spiritual life is the power to descend; if we have power to rise only, something is wrong. It is a great thing to be on the mount with God, but a man only gets there in order that afterwards he may get down among the devil-possessed and lift them up. We are not built for the mountains and the dawns and aesthetic affinities; those are for moments of inspiration, that is all. We are built for the valley, for the ordinary stuff we are in, and that is where we have to prove our mettle.[2]

Yet the time is coming when the brief taste of the presence of God experienced on a Personal Retreat will be ours forever. Spurgeon reflects:

If it is wonderful to see Him here now and then, how marvelous it will be to gaze on His blessed face forever. Never a cloud to come between, never to turn away and look at a world of weariness and woe! Blessed day! When will you dawn? Rise unsetting sun![3]

Maybe I'll see you someday on a Personal Retreat on some mountaintop or by some lake or stream. I'll recognize you sitting there at the picnic table reading the Bible and furiously writing in your journal or walking to no place in particular in deep contemplation of the wonders around you. But I won't interrupt your "face to face" encounter with God, for it is your special time. I'll just observe from a distance, offering a quick prayer of thanksgiving for the privilege of touching your life.

Face to Face

Notes

CHAPTER 1

1. Pascal, Blaise, *Pensees*, Section VII, "Morality and Doctrine," #425 Second Part.

2. Crabb, Larry, *Shattered Dreams: God's Pathway to Unexpected Joy*, (Colorado Springs: WaterBrook Press, 2001), 191.

3. Warren, Rick, *The Purpose Driven Life*, (Grand Rapids: Zondervan, 2002), 177.

4. Phillips, J. B., *The New Testament in Modern English*, (New York: Macmillan, 1958).

5. Charnock, Stephen, as quoted in Pink, Arthur. W., *The Nature of God*, (Chicago: Moody, 1975), 53.

6. Lewis, C. S., *The Lion, The Witch & the Wardrobe*, (London: Geoffrey Bles, 1950), Republished by Harper Collins, 148.

7. Ibid., 193-94.

8. Bennett, Arthur, Editor, "Divine Support", *The Valley of Vision*, (Carlisle, PA: The Banner of Truth Trust, 1975), 213.

2

Sir Charles, *Sir Charles Grandison*, Vol. 2, Letter 3, (Oxford: Oxford University Press, 1972).

2. Ehrenreich, Barbara, "The Cult of Busyness," *The Worst Years of Our Lives: Irreverent Notes from a Decade of Greed*, 1991.

3. Warren, Rick, *The Purpose Driven Life*, (Grand Rapids: Zondervan, 2002), 125.

4. Bennett, Arthur, Editor, "Evening Prayer", *The Valley of Vision*, (Carlisle, PA: The Banner of Truth Trust, 1975), 223.

5. Thoreau, Henry David, *A Week on the Concord and Merrimack Rivers (1849)* in *The Writings of Henry David Thoreau*, (New York: Houghton Mifflin, 1906), Vol. 1, 385-386.

CHAPTER 3

1. *American Heritage Dictionary* on yahoo.com.

2. Crabb, Larry, *Shattered Dreams: God's Unexpected Pathway to Joy* (Colorado Springs: WaterBrook Press, 2001), 100.

3. *America Heritage Dictionary*

4. Ibid.

5. Warren, Rick, *The Purpose Driven Life,* (Grand Rapids: Zondervan, 2002), 90.

6. *American Heritage Dictionary*

7. Ibid.

8. Thoreau, Henry David, *The Writings of Henry David Thoreau, Vol 2,* (New York: Houghton Mifflin, 1906), 148.

9. http://www.intouch.org/myintouch/mighty/portraits/ab_simpson_213600.html

10. Hillman, Os, *TGIF: Today God is First,* (Shippensburg, PA: Destiny Image, 2000), 311-312.

11. Rowland, Bruce, *Return to Snowy River Part II*, Walt Disney Company and Homeward Production, Inc., 1988; Distributed by MCA Distributing Corporation, Universal City, CA.

12. As quoted in MacMurrary, John, *The Call of Creation* (Eagle Creek, OR: Creation Calendars, 2005), 34.

13. Ibid., back cover.

CHAPTER 4

1. Spurgeon, Charles, *Morning and Evening,* (Nashville: Thomas Nelson, 1994), April 4th Evening.

2. Hendricks, Howard G., *Elijah: Confrontation, Conflict & Crisis*, (Chicago: Moody Press, 1972), 57.

3. Idid. 59-60.

4. Pfeiffer, Charles F. and Harrison, Everett F, Editors, *The Wycliffe Bible Commentary*, (Chicago: Moody Press, 1962).

CHAPTER 5

1. Sproul, R. C., *Essential Truths of the Christian Faith*, (Wheaton: Tyndale House, 1992), 82.

2. Ibid., 81.

3. Williams, Charles B., *The New Testament in the Language of the People*, (Chicago: Moody Press, 1963).

4. Spurgeon, Charles H., *Morning and Evening*, (Nashville: Thomas Nelson, 1994), November 12, Evening.

5. Henry, Matthew, *Commentary on the Whole Bible*, Matthew 14:22-33 (Wilmington: Sovereign Grace, 1972).

6. Jamieson, Robert, Fausset, A. R., & Brown, David, *Commentary Practical and Explanatory on the Whole Bible*, (Grand Rapids: Zondervan, 1961), 1002.

CHAPTER 6

1. *American Heritage Dictionary* on yahoo.com.

2. Delacroix, Eugene (1798-1863), French artist. September 3, 1922 entry, *The Journal of Eugene Delacroix*, translated by Walter Pach (1937) as found on yahoo.com.

3. Blanchot, Maurice, "The Essential Solitude," *The Space of Literature*, 1955, as quoted on yahoo.com.

4. Boswell, James (1740-1795), *Life of Johnson*, "30 March 1778," (Oxford: Oxford University Press, 1980), 898; as quoted on yahoo.com.

5. Burney, Frances (1752-1840), *The Early Journals and Letters of Fanny Burney*, journal entry March 27, 1768, (Oxford: Oxford University Press, 1988) Vol. 1, p. 1, as quoted on yahoo.com.

CHAPTER 7

1. Eldredge, John, *The Way of the Wild Heart*, (Nashville: Nelson Books, 2006), 23.

2. *Westminster Confession of Faith* (1646), Chapter III, "Of God's Eternal Decree", Section I.

3. Chambers, Oswald, *My Utmost for His Highest,* August 28th, (Grand Rapids: Discovery House, 1963).

4. Ibid.

5. Ibid., August 6th.

6. Bennett, Arthur, Editor, "Living by Prayer", *The Valley of Vision*, (Carlisle, PA: The Banner of Truth Trust, 1975), 266-267.

7. Murray, Andrew, *The Secret of Adoration*, as quoted in Edman, V. Raymond, *They Found the Secret*, (Grand Rapids: Zondervan, 1984), 118.

8. Packer, J. I., *Knowing God*, (Downers Grove, Illinois: InterVarsity Press, 1973), 23.

9. Spurgeon, Charles, *Morning and Evening,* (Nashville: Thomas Nelson, 1994), October 12th Morning.

CHAPTER 8

1. Wallis, Arthur, *God's Chosen* Fast, (Fort Washington, Pennsylvania: Christian Literature Crusade, 1968).

2. Ibid., 9.

3. Ibid., 83.

4. Ibid., 83.

5. Cott, Allan M.D., *Fasting: The Ultimate Diet*, (New York: Bantam Books, 1975), 62.

6. Ibid., 34.

CHAPTER 9

1. Chambers, Oswald, *My Utmost for His Highest,* January 13th, (Grand Rapids: Discovery House, 1963).

2. Ibid., August 19th.

3. Ibid., February 10th.

4. Matthew, Iain, *The Impact of God*, (London: Hodder and Stoughton, 1955), 71, as quoted in Crabb, Larry, *Shattered Dreams: God's Unexpected Pathway to Joy*, (Colorado Springs: WaterBrook Press, 2001), 108.

5. Warren, Rick, *The Purpose Driven Life,* (Grand Rapids: Zondervan, 2002), 90.

6. Hansel, Tim, *You Gotta Keep Dancin'*, (Elgin, IL: David C. Cook, 1985) 55.

7. Crabb, Larry, *Men & Women: Enjoying the Difference*, (Grand Rapids: Zondervan, 1991).

CHAPTER 10

1. Eldredge, John, *Waking the Dead*, (Nashville: Thomas Nelson, 2003), 84.

2. Ibid., 47.

3. Ibid., 24.

4. Hillman, Os, *Today God is First*, (Shippensburg, PA: Destiny Image, 2000), 218-219.

5. Eldredge, 48.

6. Ibid., 50.

7. Ibid., 188.

8. Hillman, 220.

9. Eldredge, 36.

10. Eldredge, John, *Wild at Heart*, (Nashville: Thomas Nelson, 2001), 36.

11. Ibid., 39.

12. Ibid., 51.

13. Ibid., 112.

14. Ibid., 132.

15. Ibid., 133.

16. Ibid., 200 quoting Gil Bailie.

17. Ibid., 206.

CONCLUSION

1. Spurgeon, Charles H., *Morning & Evening,* November 23, Evening, (Nashville: Thomas Nelson, 1994).

2. Chambers, Oswald, *My Utmost for His Highest,* October 1st, (Uhrichsville, OH: Barbour Books, 1963).

3. Spurgeon, December 10, Morning.

About the Author

After growing up in the Midwest, Monte Kline came to the Pacific Northwest in pursuit of a college education in geology and to enjoy the region's scenic beauty. However, coming to know Christ his sophomore year changed his plans, redirecting him after graduation into several years of college campus Christian ministry. During that time he developed a serious cancer condition that was ultimately resolved with a natural medicine approach. This experience launched him into a career of speaking, writing books and presenting health and nutrition from a biblical perspective, including *Eat, Drink & Be Ready*, *The Junk Food Withdrawal Manual*, *Vitamin Manual for the Confused*, *The Sick & Tired Manual*, *Body, Mind & Health*. After completing a graduate degree in Nutrition & Wholistic Health Sciences, Monte went into practice as a Clinical Nutritionist in 1984. He currently directs several of his Pacific Health Center practices throughout the Northwest.

Going back to his first hikes in the Cascade Range as a college student, Monte became fascinated with experiencing the presence of God through his creation. Over the past fifteen years he has followed God's promptings to go away alone for both short and long "personal retreats," discovering both comfort from adversity and specific life direction. From his personal experience and study of this concept in the Bible, Monte has compiled in this book what it takes to encounter God "face to face."

Monte, along with his wife Nancy and daughter Leah live on small ranch near Sisters, Oregon. To learn more about personal retreats and share your own retreat experiences, visit his **Personal Retreat Blog** at: www.personalretreat. wordpress.com.

Monte may be contacted regarding speaking engagements or his clinical practice at drkline@pacifichealthcenter.com or Pacific Health Center, PO Box 1066, Sisters, OR 97759.

Intermedia Publishing Group

Publishing That Works For You

Do you need a speaker?

Do you want Monte Kline to speak to your group or event? Then contact Larry Davis at: (623) 337-8710 or email: ldavis@intermediapr.com or use the contact form at: www.intermediapr.com.

Whether you want to purchase bulk copies of *Face To Face* or buy another book for a friend, get it now at: www.imprbooks.com.

If you have a book that you would like to publish, contact Terry Whalin, Publisher, at Intermedia Publishing Group, (623) 337-8710 or email: twhalin@intermediapub.com or use the contact form at: www.intermediapub.com.